Staffordshire Library and Information Service

Please return or renew or

TAMWORTH LIBRA

D0334808

If not required by other readers, this item may be renewed
in person, by post or telephone, online or by email.
To renew, either the book or ticket are required

**24 Hour Renewal Line
0845 33 00 740**

Staffordshire
County Council

3 8014 05127 1341

Making History
at London 2012

Making History at London 2012

25 iconic moments of the Olympic and Paralympic Games

Edited by
Brendan Gallagher

WILEY

Contents

'No other Games have come close in atmosphere, setting, enjoyment and sporting endeavour, or in modesty complemented by a magnificent, understated grandeur.'

Brendan Gallagher

Introduction

It will probably take years for the brain fully to digest the London 2012 Olympic and Paralympic Games. The pictures, stories and emotions hit us in tidal waves and there was simply too much to take in and fully appreciate at one sitting. I was already staggering about in a daze of wonder midway through the first week of the Olympic Games, and there was still so much to come. We lived the summer of 2012 in fast forward, relishing the glorious sensory overload. Only now can we begin to rewind a little, retrace our steps and reflect more clearly on those halcyon days – a delightful process that I hope this collection of articles will enhance.

Even as a wordsmith I concede that it is the flashback images that hit you first, brilliantly captured by our photographic colleagues or those covering the events for television. Here are the first five that enter my mind as I write these words – a random selection; I would probably list an entirely different five tomorrow. Ben Ainslie warning that making him angry was a big mistake; former F1 star Alessandro Zanardi, now a double amputee, bellowing out the Italian national anthem at Brands Hatch after his win in the men's Road Race – H4; director Danny Boyle's inspired transformation of Britain's green and pleasant land into a belching industrial powerhouse at the Olympic Games Opening Ceremony; Royal Marine Commando Joe Townsend, another double amputee, coming down that zipwire from the Orbit to deliver the Flame at the

Paralympic Games Opening Ceremony; Nicola Adams bursting with pride and delight after taking the first ever women's Olympic Fly Weight Boxing gold.

Yet the written word plays its part as well. It can relate what sometimes the camera does not, or cannot, see. It can expand on the background of a story and offer greater understanding of personalities involved, and consider the emotions that you can sense but not quantify. I am sure the events in this book will strike a chord, either chiming with something you noticed yourself or perhaps highlighting something that had escaped your attention first time around. There was just so much to take in, and there still is. As ever, the greatest challenge lies in deciding what to leave out.

In one sense every Olympic and Paralympic Games is unique and remarkable – as expected when you gather the 'best of the best' from around the planet every four years. World records will fall as night follows day, and the outer limits of what mankind can achieve physically will be pushed back yet again. The London 2012 Games, though, were very different and special in a way that is worth exploring. These were the 'People's Games', displaying a chemistry and sympathy between athlete and spectators that I have never witnessed before in 30 years of sports writing. The British sporting public, the most knowledge-able across the board and passionate in the world, wanted more than anything for these Games to succeed. Once their voice was heard, London 2012 soared to new heights, with the crowds and the city itself taking a starring role.

No praise can be too high for the way the home fans made every event an occasion, every heat a final. I was head down working at the Velodrome one morning when there was an earth-shattering roar. Instinctively I looked up, assuming that something wondrous had just been achieved by a British competitor. Instead I discovered that a Paralympic cyclist from Cuba with no hands and virtually no arms had just broken his personal best in the 1km Time Trial. The British fans lived and breathed every last moment with the competitors, and in very real sense became Olympians themselves. As a patriot I was immensely proud of all our competitors and medallists, but the greatest pride of all was reserved for the way in which the British public effortlessly made every athlete feel they were competing for them.

The other undoubted stars of London 2012 were the Games Makers, the 70,000 or so volunteers who gave freely of their time and were extraordinary in their dedication and sense of service. Everybody who attended the Games has their personal memories of these heroes, so I will share my favourite with you. After the last night of Paralympic action at the Velodrome, a good two hours after the public had said its final farewell to possibly the most extraordinary venue of all, myself and two colleagues were sitting high up in the press tribunes filing our final pieces. It was deserted. You could have heard a pin drop and, if the truth be told, we were all feeling a little bereft as well as completely exhausted. Suddenly that unmistakeable Heather Small anthem *Proud* fired up on the sound system: 'What have you done today to make you feel proud?' It was followed by the Velodrome announcer who had stayed to welcome the Games Makers into the arena for a special presentation ceremony. Miraculously they appeared, all 400 of them who had done service throughout the Olympic and Paralympic Games, spilling out of the tunnels and steps. Suddenly the Velodrome was alive again.

An official from LOCOG, the Organising Committee of the Olympic and Paralympic Games, made a brief, heartfelt speech, after which everybody was called forward in turn to receive a 'thank you' gold badge from the IOC and IPC. No gold medal winners at the Games could have been more delighted. As the presentations continued the DJ played a continuous loop of music that included *Magic Moments* by Perry Como and *How Deep is Your Love* by the Bee Gees. Then the Games Makers, many of whom hadn't actually set foot in the arena before, having been manning doors and lifts, printing results sheets and so on, explored the Velodrome with delight. They took their shoes off, slid down the steep slopes and staged foot races around the bottom of the track. For a splendid 15 minutes or so they not so much took the stage as owned it. I'm not sure that little cameo wasn't my abiding memory of the entire Games. The pleasure of it all certainly brought a tear to the eye.

So what memories and thoughts do we hope to rekindle and perhaps tease out for you in this volume? Hopefully many and varied, from outstanding individuals to the genesis and genius of the Olympic Park and the iconic venues that we grew to love and take great pride in. A radical emphasis on sustainability, combined with a bold yet intimate approach to architecture and design, created a succession of innovative structures, some permanent, some temporary. From the poised Velodrome and elegant, economical Olympic Stadium to the gleaming Water Polo Arena and magnificent Greenwich Park arena, the venues and their city became active participants in the Games' energy and drama. The Opening and Closing Ceremonies relished the big stage of the Olympic Stadium, presenting thought-provoking, powerful, occasionally comedic spectacles with a quintessentially British feel. They captured the nation's imagination, providing a magnificent lead-in to the Games and revealing Britain's huge talent for design, style and innovation to a global audience of over one billion. For athletes such as Peter Norfolk, the chance to be the first British Flagbearer to lead ParalympicsGB into the tumultuous applause of a home crowd was a highlight of an extraordinarily successful career.

Every journey starts with a single step, so we will also rewind the clock a little and look at how London won the race to host the Games. It is a success story well worth repeating because the bid's attention to detail and clear concept of how the Olympic and Paralympic Games would look underpinned everything that followed. Rarely has a Host Nation been more faithful to its promises and commitments. The Games that Lord Coe, Sir Keith Mills and others envisaged were the Games that London actually delivered. The triumphant and emotional passage of the Olympic Flame around the UK was an early indicator in the build-up to the Games that something very special was happening. Despite the wet weather, crowds came out to see the Olympic Flame pass: the British public were on board. They came out again in August to support the Paralympic Torch Relay, bringing the Flame lit on Great Britain and Northern Ireland's highest mountain peaks from Stoke Mandeville, the heartland of the Paralympic Games, to the Stadium in the Olympic Park.

The London 2012 Festival offered a spectacular variety of cultural treats, from global festivals such as the BT River of Music, reflecting the huge diversity of countries participating at the Olympic and Paralympic Games, to inspirational theatre, dance, art installations and pop-up performance. The World Shakespeare Festival, the biggest-ever celebration of Shakespeare's work, mounted 70 productions at the home of the Royal Shakespeare Company in Stratford-upon-Avon and across the UK. In London the Globe Theatre, reconstructed on its original site by the Thames, held performances of all 37 of Shakespeare's plays in 37 languages. At the heart of this blaze of artistic activity was the desire to inspire the next generation and to provide a change of pace, an opportunity for visitors to kick back and relax a little during an incredible summer of sport.

For the second Olympic Games in succession, Usain Bolt was the first name on our lips as he repeated his sprint hat-trick from Beijing 2008 – the 100m, 200m and 4 x 100m Relay. Outwardly the Jamaican never seems to change; life is still a disco and a party to enjoy, but you do not achieve his level of greatness without inner steel and conviction. The word pre-Games was that he had a slight back problem and wasn't quite at his best, that compatriot Yohan Blake was the next big thing, that an upset was in the air. All of the above may have been true, but Bolt revealed himself to be a true champion. He remains the fastest man in the history of the world and when he hit the turbo 50m into the 100m final, it was a moment to behold. He is still 'the man'.

Michael Phelps of the USA is a star of the same magnitude, bravely putting his reputation and body on the line against young tyros eager for a scalp. It wasn't an easy ride, and there were occasions when age appeared to be catching up with the champion, but the remarkable swimmer rallied to leave London 2012 as the most decorated Olympian of all time, including winning the most Olympic gold medals. For an astonishing third Olympic

Games in succession Phelps provided the narrative for a hugely successful Swimming meet.

From a momentous 'first' in one of the Olympic Games' oldest sports (Swimming featured in the 1896 Olympic Games) on to one of the newest, making a long overdue debut at London 2012. For the first time women's Boxing featured on the programme and, as many of those involved had predicted, the competitors' skill, agility and charisma won over many new fans. For Britons Natasha Jonas, the first British woman to win an Olympic Boxing match, and Nicola Adams, who went on to take a stunning Fly Weight gold, it was an inspirational development that has transformed their sport; the focus now is on Rio 2016.

A true champion and global figure in a different sphere is Britain's Ben Ainslie, bidding to become only the fourth Olympian to win individual gold at four consecutive Games. Rather like Bolt, Ainslie seemed a little vulnerable going into the Sailing competition. A serious back injury had required surgery pre-Games and was still giving pain, and he had struggled to win selection over several talented domestic rivals. Then he started poorly down at Weymouth and Portland, enabling an outstanding opponent to start building a dangerous lead. Again 'what happened next' makes for a fascinating read and reveals exactly why Ainslie is now considered the greatest sailor in Olympic history.

On the subject of Holy Grails, Bradley Wiggins arrived at the Olympic Games fresh, if that's the right word, from his historic victory at the Tour de France – the first time a British rider had won the world's greatest endurance race. Could he raise his game? He proved he could – and with real style, his loveable, quirky and very British character utterly charming the home crowd. Wiggins is surely the first British sportsman identifiable by his side-burns alone, although wicketkeeper Godfrey Evans probably runs him close. Cycling again provided a rich source of medals, stories and drama at both Games, captivating a sporting nation that has embraced the sport fully over the last decade or so. In the Velodrome Sir Chris Hoy and Victoria Pendleton departed from the Olympic arena one last time with more gold medals, but the bigger story was how, against all the odds, Great Britain matched their Beijing 2008 record of seven gold medals on the track. The Track Cycling programme had been radically altered, nations restricted to just one rider per event and the world had raised their game. There would be no repeat of the 'Great Haul of China', everyone said. Wrong. Gloriously wrong.

One competitor under huge pressure all summer was Jessica Ennis. Being a poster girl for an Olympic Games can be a poisoned chalice, and immensely stressful as well. Ennis delivered magnificently, however, with many citing the roar from 80,000 fans that greeted her as she lined up for the 100m hurdles, the first Heptathlon event, early on Friday morning as their favourite moment of the Games. On the podium with her gold medal she managed that famous smile, even as she became distinctly tearful with the relief of it all. Fifteen million viewers looking on at home were dabbing their eyes as well.

Mo Farah was another who showed extraordinary grace under pressure. He first took gold in the 10,000m and then won the 5000m on 'Super Saturday', a remarkable triumph complementing Ennis and Greg Rutherford in the Long Jump. All great Olympians work hard, even those who claim not to, but nobody surely can have trained harder in the lead-up to London 2012 than Farah, as he roamed the world looking for the perfect environment. At one stage his form dipped a little – he was overdoing it, we were told. Yet his self-belief never faltered, and come London 2012 he was ready. Imperious, engaging and modest at all times, a devoted family man with a laddish streak, he ticked all the boxes for an army of fans. His celebratory 'Mobot' is with us forever now – he's even got Bolt copying him.

In terms of star individuals the Paralympic Games was no different. How could it be otherwise as we grew to understand the events more and to appreciate the journeys of those involved? Before London 2012 David Weir was a legendary figure in the world of Paralympic sport and a regular winner of the London Marathon; now he is a legendary sporting figure, period. His four races, all leading to gold medals, encompassed every quality we love in our sporting heroes and every tactical nuance that goes into racing. The same applies to Sarah Storey in the Track and Road Cycling, another four-time gold medal winner and an athlete so talented that she was almost competing at the Olympic Games two weeks earlier – she was the last rider to be cut from Great Britain's world-beating Team Pursuit squad. And it was another remarkable Games for Ellie Simmonds, the teenager who stole the nation's hearts at Beijing 2008 – then did it all over again four years later. A brilliant swimmer with an infectious personality, she lit up our screens in 2012, winning a further four medals, two golds, a silver and a bronze, in a brilliant and mature display. Down at Greenwich Park Sophie Christiansen, another strong and delightful personality, dazzled spectators with a bold and innovative dressage music freestyle routine. Technically challenging and perfectly executed, it was to bring Christiansen her third gold medal at her third Paralympic Games.

New Paralympians also captivated crowds at the Games. On 'Thrilling Thursday' (7 September 2012) the young British sprinting star Jonnie Peacock won a highly charged 100m – T44, defeating the legendary Oscar Pistorius and 200m – T44 champion Alan Fonteles Cardoso Oliveira in the process. Many other young competitors, such as Hannah Cockroft, Paul Blake, Beverley Jones and Ola Abidogun, took medals, and so many of their teammates achieved personal bests on the greatest stage. The Games also introduced British spectators to less familiar sports such as Boccia. A dramatic bronze medal match in the Team – BC1/BC2 competition saw Great Britain's Daniel Bentley, Nigel Murray and David Smith narrowly defeat Portugal in a cauldron of intense excitement that delighted the exuberant crowd.

Selfless teamwork is a massive part of sport and we examine the nuances and glory of that in some depth. Inspirational Hockey caption Katie Walsh had the ill luck to suffer a fractured jaw in her team's first match against Japan. A successful operation and great personal courage saw her return, wearing plates and a face mask, to lead her team on to a magnificent bronze.

Rowing is one of the ultimate team sports in every sense, which has been acknowledged for decades, and London 2012 proved an outstanding regatta. Great Britain, who had never previously won a gold medal in women's events, secured not one but three, and the Team GB men's Four also took a brilliant gold – just part of the team's great contribution to the Games. And what of the team dynamic in Paralympic Cycling's tandem events, when a 'sighted pilot' guides the visually impaired 'stoker' around the course? Aileen McGlynn and her new pilot, Helen Scott, did not have everything their own way in the

Velodrome at London 2012, but they nonetheless found a way to triumph in front of a delirious home crowd.

And what of the Jumping Team Competition down at the majestic Greenwich Park arena – an event in which riders must not only work with one another for the common good, but have also to earn trust and respect from their horses? And then, despite the team ethic, the burden of responsibility sometimes falls on just one competitor, as Great Britain's Peter Charles discovered. I won't exhaust the list here; there are too many stories waiting for you to explore.

While these memories come rushing back to us in a glorious tangle, an overall assessment is rather easier, both in relation to other London Games and the wider history of the modern Games. IOC President Jacques Rogge called the Olympic Games 'happy and glorious', and Sir Philip Craven insisted that the Paralympic Games were the 'greatest ever'. Lord Coe, summing up the entire summer, proudly claimed that both events were stamped 'Made in Britain' in perpetuity. Great movers and shakers tend to choose their words carefully. Infinitely lower down the scale, I would simply declare them the greatest Olympic and Paralympic Games ever, by a country mile. No other Games have come close in atmosphere, setting, enjoyment and sporting endeavour, or in modesty complemented by a magnificent, understated grandeur.

Trying to step back a little and be objective, London 2012, to these eyes, straddled the two extremes of the cash-rich 1908 Games, designed to showcase imperial prestige, and the 'Austerity Games' of 1948, and that was another factor that made them superb. London is the first city on Earth to stage three Olympic Games, and it drew on past experience to present a confident, joyful 21st-century event. The wonderful hospitality that, within the limits of rationing, had characterised London 1948 was still in evidence, but this time there was to be a conscious, carefully crafted legacy in sport and beyond. The 1948 Olympic Games, hosted on a shoestring by a country still shattered by war, had provided no physical legacy – one of many reasons why British Olympic sport struggled in the decades after 1948. There were no sparkling new national stadia nor any fresh investment in sports that had perhaps been struggling. Nor was there a significant sporting legacy, with just three gold medals to reflect on and to inspire a nation in the post-war years.

There was, however, one very notable exception. On Wednesday 28 July 1948, the day before the Opening Ceremony of the Olympic Games at Wembley Stadium, 16 disabled athletes gathered at the spinal unit at the Stoke Mandeville Hospital just outside Aylesbury. Here they held their own 'Olympic Games', the Stoke Mandeville Games for the Paralysed, based largely on archery and club throwing. The seeds of the Paralympic movement were being sown – one of Great Britain's most splendid gifts to the world, and one that has also benefitted so many in this country.

Which brings us back to London 2012, the perfect amalgamation of everything Great Britain has learned from its long involvement in the modern Olympic and Paralympic Movement, including the hosting of two previous Olympic Games. Those of London 2012 were meticulously organised and staged, but in an unfussy way that enabled them to be generous, welcoming and warm-hearted towards everybody – and with that atmosphere established, the world's great athletes relaxed and performed. In ambience and enjoyment the London 2012 Olympic and Paralympic Games felt more like the much smaller and intimate Commonwealth Games, a remarkable trick to pull off. Security was there, of course, every second of every day, keeping the sporting world safe and happy, but it often seemed virtually invisible. An insanely difficult job, magnificently executed by all those concerned.

The Olympic Park was incredible, and away from it London and its surrounds have never looked better. An immense contribution was made by Hyde Park, The Mall, Wimbledon, Greenwich Park, North Greenwich Arena, Eton Dorney, Hampton Court Palace, Box Hill, Weymouth and Portland – and Brands Hatch, which nearly stole the show right at the end. The transport system worked beautifully, far better than expected and even the weather behaved itself. As you enjoy this book I'm sure you will feel, as I do, that the London 2012 Olympic and Paralympic Games were truly blessed. Yet the greatest blessing of all is that we in this country were granted the privilege, first of staging them and then of offering our support.

Brendan Gallagher

'For the first time in 18 months of design work, the Park had now come to life in this studio for us all to see.'

Kevin Owens

1
PREPARING FOR LONDON 2012

Bringing the Games Home

The Plasticine Park

Bringing the Games Home

Brendan Gallagher

*How Great Britain conceived and won the bid
for London 2012*

Jason Queally was the man who first served notice of the new sporting 'Cool Britannia' that was to set the country on track for the London 2012 Games. I can remember that early morning vividly. It was 16 September, the first day proper of the Sydney 2000 Games, and I was driving to Leicester for a rugby match when I pulled over for petrol with Radio 5 on. It was the final stages of the men's 1km Time Trial at the Sydney Velodrome, and the forecourt at Watford Gap services came to a halt as a dozen drivers or more, similarly tuned in, refused to get out until Queally had been confirmed as the winner. Cue a volley of horns and loud cheering – very un-British, but all rather cheering and a seminal moment. British sport, after several years of underachievement, had struck back.

Remarkably it was only four years since its nadir, or its wake-up call for those of a more positive disposition. The Atlanta 1996 Games, in which Team GB garnered just one gold medal, was, along with Helsinki 1952, Great Britain's poorest ever return from the event. Out of 300 competitors, only Sir Steve Redgrave and Matthew Pinsent returned from the USA as winners. Yet in truth this low ebb was the moment when the journey to London 2012 began. From that moment onwards the only direction left was upwards.

For a while, not so very long ago, our champions were chronically underfunded and achieved great things despite the system. Professionalism had become a fact of life in all the other major sporting nations, yet Great Britain remained absorbed by the amateur ethos. For some that was a genuine ideological choice, but increasingly it began to smack of a convenient excuse.

Initially all that mattered was for our 'athletes' in all sports to start competing on a level playing field. Happily a solution was already in the pipeline in the form of funding from the National Lottery. Introduced in 1994, its impact, both short- and longer-term, was dramatic. And it is probable that, without the Lottery and the instigation of Lottery funding, London's dream of holding an Olympic and Paralympic Games would not have been fulfilled.

Most 'experts' believed that few benefits would be seen by the public before the Athens 2004 Games, working on the assumption that sports training, rather like an ocean liner, takes time to slow down, turn round and head off in a better direction. But they were unduly pessimistic. The 'Lottery effect' was immediate, with morale improving instantly as a generation suddenly felt appreciated by the nation they had made great sacrifices already to represent. Never underestimate what Lottery funding brought to the table. The change gave sportsmen and women the opportunity to attend funded camps and to train full-time; it also meant that coaches could be supported in a similar fashion and provide the expert medical, nutritional and conditioning support required.

Elite sportsmen and women could now make a lifestyle

choice. If they wanted to pursue sporting excellence they might not make a fortune, but they no longer had to sell the family silver or hawk themselves around for handouts to do so. Results at Sydney 2000 spoke for themselves. After the disappointment of Atlanta 1996, the medals started to flow with pleasing regularity. Our sportsmen and women were 'ball-park' again. Great Britain brought home 11 gold medals from Sydney 2000 in seven different sports: Athletics, Boxing, Cycling, Modern Pentathlon, Rowing, Sailing and Shooting.

Fast forward to Manchester and August 2002 and another vital stepping stone. Here, for the first time in decades, we were provided with concrete evidence that Great Britain might stage a major sporting event again. To these eyes Manchester totally embraced the Commonwealth Games and unexpectedly made them into something very special. I remember one evening, within the space of five or six hours, watching a brilliant squash final between Britain's Peter Nicol and Canada's Jonathan Power, nipping over to a packed Velodrome to witness Australia beat Great Britain and break the world record in the men's Team Pursuit and then walking over to the City of Manchester Stadium where a capacity crowd of 39,000 were enjoying another outstanding night of athletics. The facilities and performances were world-class and the crowd involvement could not have been better. This was top drawer.

As the Commonwealth Games drew to a close a number of enlightened administrators and opinion-makers – still a minority, but influential nonetheless – started to ask the inevitable question. 'Why not? Why shouldn't Great Britain put in another Olympic bid?' Chief among them was Simon Clegg who, as CEO of the British Olympic Association (BOA), had never given up on the idea of another 'British' Games. A detailed 400-page plan for a potential 2012 bid already lay in his drawer. Among other things, this made a major virtue of Great Britain's commitment to the Paralympic Games, which historically has been second to none. It also recognised that there would have to be a huge commitment to 'legacy' in any serious bid. In the difficult conditions of 1948, when war-torn London essentially rescued the Games at short notice, there had been almost no Olympic legacy or upgrading of elite sporting facilities. Britain had missed out massively in that respect.

But before any Olympic bid could even be proposed, there had to be a sea change in political will and public opinion. Politicians tend to follow where the public lead, so the more astute of the pro-Olympic lobby saw that the priority was to win the public's heart and mind. Which is where David Welch, the former sports editor of the *Daily Telegraph*, entered the fray. He mobilised his large stable of broadsheet writers to undertake a concerted campaign to convince everybody concerned – the politicians, administrators and fellow opinion-makers – that Britain could and must bid again.

He was aware, in an initially sceptical climate, of the long-term benefits that hosting the Games would bring for London, for Britain and for sport of all kinds. Welch's confidence influenced others in the media and support for the bid gathered momentum. Following a survey showing that the vast majority of the British public backed the Olympic bid, Tony Blair's Labour Government was finally persuaded to get on board. Bearing in mind that governments can get badly embarrassed if bids go wrong, this was no small achievement. And another very tough decision had to be made. Manchester, the city and its citizens, admittedly played a superb hand in their staging of the 2002 Commonwealth Games, and they had also kept the British flame alive by bidding for the 1996 and 2000 Olympic and Paralympic Games, but the harsh reality was that it made no sense for them to front Great Britain's 2012 bid. Clegg clearly summed up the situation when he acknowledged, 'After Sydney was chosen at the IOC [International Olympic Committee] session in September 1993, we came home and took stock of why Manchester had not fared better. We said then that we would not bid for 2004, and the clear message from the IOC was that only London would be considered a serious contender.' Only London had the clout to stand any chance internationally of wooing the IOC delegates and winning the vote.

Bob Scott, who had headed up Manchester's two unsuccessful Olympic bids, appreciated the inevitability of this decision. 'I was aware that I was not leading the first XI,' he admitted. 'The international world thinks London when they think Great Britain. If you put up Manchester or any other city than London, however sound the bid, you cannot get over the fact that you are not London. The world then comes to the conclusion that Britain has decided to send out its second XI and is not taking the competition seriously. I found myself between a rock and a hard place.'

London might have been the obvious – the only – choice of Host City for Great Britain's 2012 bid, but convincing the city itself was not without difficulties. The then Mayor of London, Ken Livingstone, was better known for his love of amphibians than his love of sport. Years later in 2008, a speech he made at St Martin's in the Fields church in Trafalgar Square revealed his motivation behind his support. 'I bid for the Olympics because it's the only way to get the billions of pounds out of the Government to develop the East End,' Livingstone explained. If London was going to bid for the Games it would demand not only a sporting legacy but also cleaner soil, a better infrastructure and more housing for people living in some of the most deprived boroughs in the city.

Already the targets for London 2012 were being mapped out. Certainly there needed to be a huge investment in sport – both in venues and people – to give today's sportsmen and women every opportunity and to inspire the generation of tomorrow. The city, too, would be transformed. A huge area of east London that had been used for industry and landfill for centuries would become a stunning, environmentally conscious new park. Transport links would be improved, new homes built and jobs created. New standards in sustainability would also be set, to change building practices nationwide.

In June 2003 the American businesswoman Barbara Cassani was made bid leader. At the time the appointment was met with some surprise, but it was a deliberate attempt to establish sound economic principles before the politics and 'selling' of the bid took over. In retrospect Lord Coe's succeeding Cassani in that role in May 2004 seems entirely logical, with his contacts and influence adding significant weight to the bid. It combined emphasis on Britain's historic contribution to the Olympic Games and its deep-rooted Paralympic associations with a commitment to inspire young people around the world, underlined with clear and public government support.

Six months later Coe and his team handed over the 600-page candidature file to the IOC in Lausanne. 'Our vision for the Olympic and Paralympic Games in London in 2012 is clear,' said Coe as he handed over the weighty document. 'It is to create the best Games the world has ever seen by unlocking the UK's unrivalled passion for sport, by delivering the best Games for athletes to compete in, by showcasing London's unmatched cultural wealth and diversity and by creating a real and lasting legacy. Our vision is a Games that will inspire, excite, engage and be owned by the next generation. Games that fully reflect the IOC's new thinking – excellence without extravagance.'

When the IOC met at the Raffles convention centre in Singapore between 4 and 6 July 2005 to vote on who should host the 2012 Games, Paris was favourite to win. Four other cities were still in the running: London, Madrid, New York City and Moscow. Coe knew that the race was going to be very close and that the final lobbying and presentations in Singapore were going to be vital. He put together an extraordinary bid party. The then Prime Minister, Tony Blair, spoke to an estimated 40 delegates in person before flying back to Scotland to host a G8 meeting. The great and the good of British Olympic and Paralympic Games history – Steve Redgrave, Daley Thompson, Tanni Grey-Thompson, David Hemery and others, plus sporting heroes such as David Beckham – showed their absolute commitment to bringing the Games home. But this bid was not just a gathering of Great Britain's sporting glitterati. Of the 100 personnel each bid country was allocated for the lobbying and presentation, Coe chose to include 30 east London school children. When it came to his personal message in London's presentation, he focused in on the young, of both Britain and the world. This had to be an Olympic and Paralympic Games that captured their imagination. He spoke from his heart, not the autocue, and the IOC delegates seemed to like what they heard very much.

'When I was 12 … I was marched into a large school hall with my classmates. We sat in front of an ancient, black-and-white TV and watched grainy pictures from the Mexico City Olympic Games,' he told the delegates. 'Two athletes from our home town were competing. John Sherwood won a bronze medal in the 400m Hurdles. His wife Sheila just narrowly missed gold in the Long Jump. That day a window to a new world opened for me. By the time I was back in my classroom, I knew what I wanted to do and what I wanted to be … Thirty-five years on, I stand before you with those memories still fresh. Still inspired by this great Movement.'

The process was relatively simple given the momentous nature of the vote. Each of the 104 eligible IOC delegates would take part in a series of secret ballots. After each ballot, if no candidate city had gained an absolute majority of 50 per cent or more of the votes cast, the city with the fewest votes would drop out and another ballot or round would be held. Initially London, Paris and Madrid were neck and neck while Moscow was the first to drop out, having polled 15 votes. New York dropped out in round two with 16 votes, but Madrid picked up more of the Russian vote than anybody else and thus topped the polling – 32 plays London's 27 and Paris 25. This was going to be very close.

The top three candidates had made it through, and round three saw some interesting movement. Madrid actually lost a vote from the previous round while London moved encouragingly from 27 to 39 and Paris jumped from 25 to 33. Madrid was eliminated and round four was now a simple two-horse race, with the destination of the 'Spanish vote' a key factor. Ultimately it sided marginally with Paris who picked up 17 votes to London's 15, but it wasn't enough.

London came home in the fourth and final round, 54–50.

When IOC president Jacques Rogge announced the result at 12.49 BST on 6 July 2005, the bid team went wild with joy. Thousands of miles across the globe, in London's Trafalgar Square, the party began in earnest as Londoners celebrated the fact that the Games were returning to their city for the first time since 1948. Less then 24 hours later terrorist atrocities in London brought about the deaths of 56 people, including the four perpetrators, and injuring over 700 innocent individuals. At first the winning of the bid seemed irrelevant in the face of such an outrage, but as the capital gradually got back to normality Britain's pride in securing the Games returned. It was accompanied by a determination to do the very best job possible. In his defiant response to the bombings, Ken Livingstone explained why London would not be cowed by the attacks. 'In the days that follow look at our airports, look at our sea ports and look at our railway stations … you will see that people from the rest of Britain, people from around the world will arrive in London to become Londoners and to fulfil their dreams and achieve their potential.' Presenting a bold and undeterred country to the world now seemed more important than ever.

The city's steely determination to overcome any obstacle thrown in its way was called upon repeatedly over the next seven years. In 2008 the world was thrown into economic turmoil, but unlike 1948, when London hosted the 'Austerity Games', this couldn't be run on a principle of 'make do and mend'. Both the Olympic and Paralympic Games were a major investment, with national prestige riding on their success. In the event the Games magnificently displayed Great Britain's flair for innovation, improvisation and design, demonstrating that London truly is a city like no other.

The Plasticine Park

Kevin Owens

The challenge of creating an Olympic Park like no other from an area of dereliction and decay captured the imagination of brilliant architects and designers from the UK and beyond

For many, the moment the London 2012 Games became real was when Jacques Rogge, the President of the International Olympic Committee (IOC), opened that envelope in Singapore, and uttered the memorable words, 'The Games of the 30th Olympiad in 2012 are awarded to the city of London.' Although I was swept along by the tide of euphoria, my personal moment was a little more tangential. It was early October 2007, just over one year into my role as Design Principal for the London Organising Committee of the Olympic Games and Paralympic Games (LOCOG), when the reality of the opportunity truly began to emerge. Little did I know that an early-evening dash through the rain across London from the working site of Stratford to a spartan back-street studio in Hatton Garden would truly signify the genesis of London's Olympic Park.

As usual, I arrived fashionably late to find the landscape team, led by John Hopkins and George Hargreaves, huddled around a quite massive raw model. The anticipation was palpable. There before us were the sinuous rolling

34

forms of the future Olympic Park, blended together from masses of plasticine, folded card, found oddments and an array of brightly coloured 'drawing pin' trees. For the first time in 18 months of design work, effort and ground site work, the Park had now come to life in this studio for us all to see. These rolling forms of modelling clay, sculpted and worked by the landscape team, were soon to become the playground for the Games, and the largest new urban park in Europe for a century. The Park had elevated itself out of the computer-generated graphics and flat illustrated working plans into a sinuous curving form that was there to be shared and celebrated. It would take many more months, and plenty of midnight oil burned in the studio, but everyone there realised that our shared vision was about to become a reality.

We all knew that our success was going to be measured on a scale like never before, and so our focus very quickly centred on *why* we were doing this, rather than on what we were attempting to create. It would only be through fully understanding the why that we could realise the solution that would anchor the Games for 2012. This would involve the stitching together of brilliant minds and ideas on a timeframe that felt impossible, but with a goal that was singular, optimistic, unified and completely shared. For London 2012 to be a success, we knew it would be down to an absolute collaborative approach – a shared vision, right from the initial concepts through to the final design and delivery of our venues and the Park. This was to be a herculean combined effort between ourselves in LOCOG and, critically, our colleagues and partners in the Olympic Delivery Authority (ODA) to deliver our collective aspirations. In essence it was a small group of likeminded people with a clear vision of the goals ahead.

At the time of the playful clay model the ODA were already well advanced into the enabling works across the site. Designs were emerging for both the Olympic Stadium and the Aquatics Centre, and even much of the infrastructure of the Park, but we were still pulling the canvas that would stitch the key venues of the London 2012 Olympic and Paralympic Games together. It was a bold move by John Hopkins to introduce George Hargreaves and his team so late in the masterplanning process, but ultimately it became one of our collective masterstrokes. It gave many of us the opportunity to take stock, review the progress to date and readdress the context of the Park within the entire context of the London 2012 project. The reflective time taken at this stage would allow us to unlock our Olympian trump card. London's Olympic Park was indeed a park – not an oversized precinct to house sports venues, but a real robust London park, building on our proud heritage of the Royal Parks, reinvigorating the lost River Lea and celebrating the Games in a setting like no other.

Early design lessons learned on the Park would translate across the entire Games, and vice versa. We quickly appreciated that it was the bold simple moves that we were making here that would translate across the Games – keeping it clear, keeping it simple; opening views both near and far; drawing the city to the Park and the Park to the city; bringing sustainability to the fore; and ultimately celebrating our setting. This was a case of avoiding our British sensibilities and allowing ourselves to make a true statement of intent. There was an opportunity to bring the pomp and grandeur of London to the Park.

We had been given the challenge of designing and delivering the vision for London 2012 that was laid out in the winning bid. This promised to deliver a Games that would re-engage with youth, celebrate our nation and heritage, and ultimately refocus the Games with sport at its heart. The winning bid laid out a remarkable blueprint of what could be. Now it was down to a small, multi-discipline group of like-minded people truly to interrogate how we could do it.

I joined London 2012 at a time when the entire LOCOG architectural design team consisted of one single full-time member of staff, confronting a potential of more than 250 individual projects. Derek Wilson was attempting to jump-start the largest singular design challenge out of the blocks, but with the leanest team in history … Recognising that this was going to be a marathon rather than a sprint, our key was to invest in the right minds and people, and build on some rock-solid principles. We needed an honest, open-minded approach to the task at hand, ultimately striving for a holistic approach to design that would resonate through all our venues across the nation.

Sustainability was at the core, and would underpin much of what we would do. We understood very early on that a truly sustainably designed global event had never been achieved – rather than try to post-rationalise the efforts of previous events, we knew that we had to start from scratch. To deliver the most sustainable Olympic and Paralympic Games ever would take immense effort and a bold approach. This was unknown territory for everyone. As a design team, before considering what we would build and how we would design it, we immediately set the challenge to reduce the amount we would build to a minimum – a 25 per cent reduction on previous Games. Our Games in London utilised an incredible amount of temporary elements, over 250,000 temporary seats alone – three Wembley stadiums! No one would thank us for reducing the number of seats, but what we could do was challenge the rest of our build, and focus our energies on delivering the most spectacular sporting arenas for athlete and spectator alike.

The view from the Park bench

Inevitably a large part of our initial focus was on the Olympic Park and assisting the ODA with the design and development of the venues within. However, we also understood that many of our best wins from the bid were on the fields of our historic venues – we challenged ourselves to understand how lessons learned here could then be brought back to the Lea Valley. One thing was certain, we were creating venues and arenas in spaces and places that would not see this scale of event again for generations.

This was an exercise in humility for the design team. As good as we believed ourselves to be, we knew that we were no match for the likes of our 'incumbent' architects – notably Inigo Jones (The Queen's House, Greenwich), Sir Christopher Wren (The Old Royal Naval College, Greenwich) and William Kent (Horse Guards Parade). It was our role to celebrate these settings, and ultimately bring them into the architecture of London 2012 – but always to complement, not compete. As with most things in life, it is often the simplest solutions that work best. Derek and I brought in the brilliant bid minds of Jerry Anderson and Jeff Keas, and set out the challenge. Many hours, and reams of tracing paper, were spent reviewing, redrafting, sketching glorious ambitions for all of these sites – all generating great individual ideas, but not landing the knockout punch we were looking for. Ironically it was not in the studio at all, but on a park bench in Greenwich Park, on a rather bleak February morning, that we collectively settled upon our approach.

To put it in context, a few weeks earlier we had learned that we would have to completely review the approach that we were taking to the design of one of our blue riband venues – Equestrian at Greenwich Park. For the bid we had optimistically hoped to have crammed 23,000 people around the King Henry VIII's tilt yard in front of Inigo Jones' The Queen's House, but surveys quickly illustrated that, alas, this would not be possible without some major works. A rethink was required. We had been experiencing this across a multitude of venues including Lord's Cricket Ground, Horse Guards Parade and even on the Park itself, with the shift of the Basketball Arena and the subsequent move of Fencing to the new extended ExCeL centre.

It became immediately evident that the only place we could put the Equestrian arena was on the main lawn of Greenwich Park. We quickly responded to the formal geometry of Inigo Jones and Sir Christopher Wren's masterplans, and placed the enclosed four-sided arena directly in alignment with the historical plan. Our Equestrian stadium would provide the temporary culmination of the timeless setting. We knew it was a logical solution, and it was the right solution, but just not celebratory enough. We had still failed to capture the essence of the place.

And so to the park bench in February 2008. Four architects sat on the top of a hill, in the company of General Wolfe's statue, clutching styrene cups of strong tepid tea, trying to make out Canary Wharf in the drizzle. And then it dawned on us. A horseshoe ... not literally on the horse, but as a form for all of our main historical arenas. The simple idea was to create three-sided seating bowls that would then enable the fourth elevation to be completed by the historic or local setting. It was only by immersing ourselves in the setting (and the drizzle) that the magic emerged.

We immediately sought to apply this concept to Greenwich Park, as well as Horse Guards Parade, Lord's Cricket Ground, and even our temporary Hockey and BMX venues within the Olympic Park – all distinctly unique settings, but collectively embracing the spirit of the London Games. Rather than create inward-looking venues that focused only upon the sport within, we would seek to celebrate the sport within its setting. The look of our Games would not be thought up within some studio environment – the look was London, front and centre. Shots beamed around the world would always reference our magnificent city and nation. Building upon a clear single strategy, we would create a complete portfolio of images that would celebrate sport and our city – and this time not just for the world's cameras, as at Barcelona 1992, but for our most important constituents: athletes and spectators. It was this clear and simple vision that we would then employ across all of our venues, whether they be within our glorious new Olympic Park, Rowing at Eton Dorney or Mountain Biking at Hadleigh Farm. The setting would always be paramount.

Over the coming weeks and months we were continually surprised by the power of this clear approach. Venues that had once seemed only sport-focused now had the chance to reaffirm themselves within their settings. The cityscape provided a stunning backdrop, including some new aspects from the Park itself. On the BMX Track, as an athlete perched on the top of the imposing start ramp, adrenaline pumping, heart pounding, he or she was framed in the distance by the Velodrome. We wanted to present a constant reminder of time and place. In this way we would build on our heritage to create a new and exciting view of the future for our nation. The architecture of the Games would be anchored well and truly within the city.

One of the long-term aims of the London 2012 Games was to set a new direction for major events. We can see today that the bold ambitions for inspiring young people, legacy, accessibility and sustainability, are already filtering through to the next generation of global events. Indeed, London 2012 represents a major shift in the approach to the presentation, architecture and design of venues for the Olympic and Paralympic Games – an approach that was designed to ensure a truly memor-able Games experience for all clients, especially athletes, but anchored in an incredible post-Games legacy. While major events seek 'defining moments' to help instil memories of their event in the minds of participants, spectators and viewing audiences, often achieved through Opening Ceremonies and the great sporting achievements, London 2012 also seeks to support and enhance the experience of the Games through the design of venues and settings for the sport.

Our approach showcases sport and athletic achievement on fields of play anchored in unique settings and surroundings that reflect the context and culture of the Host City and inspire participants, spectators and viewers everywhere. As a spectator in the summer of 2012, we were afforded access to extraordinary views, venues and sights. The Games is a defining moment in our nation's history, comparable to the Great Exhibition of 1851 and the Festival of Britain in 1952. We have left our mark in the minds and hearts of all who witnessed this amazing event. Although delivered in difficult economic times, the Games has enabled us to regroup and reaffirm our pride as a nation, putting forward an optimistic and progressive view of Britain's future. A beacon for future generations.

'The long list of colourful, exciting, weird and wonderful cultural offerings from the London 2012 Festival has left poignant and joyful memories across the UK.'

Sarah Edworthy

2
THE LONDON 2012 FESTIVAL

The World Shakespeare Festival

A Festival of Hope and Glory

The World Shakespeare Festival

Vikki Orvice

This international celebration, at the heart of the London 2012 Festival, presented Shakespeare as a world playwright addressing universal human themes

The Bell that rang out around the Olympic Stadium on 27 July 2012 was heard by millions of people around the world. Weighing 27 tonnes, it is the largest harmonically tuned bell in the world, cast in London's Whitechapel Bell Foundry where Big Ben (a modest 13.5 tonnes) was made in 1856. Its peal at 9pm, sounded by 2012 Tour de France winner Bradley Wiggins, signalled the long-awaited start of the Opening Ceremony, sending a thrill of anticipation around the Olympic Stadium. The 'Isles of Wonder' theme at the Ceremony's heart was inspired by Shakespeare's *The Tempest*, and the Olympic Bell that heralded the spectacle was inscribed with a quote from Caliban's memorable speech: 'Be not afeard, the isle is full of noises'.

Mention Stratford and most people would immediately think of Shakespeare's birthplace, the small market town on the banks of the River Avon in Warwickshire. Not Stratford on the banks of the River Lea in the east end of London, a region now synonymous with the London 2012 Olympic and Paralympic Games. But it seems appropriate that the two Stratfords, one the spiritual heartland of

Shakespeare, the other an emotional and physical cauldron of 21st-century sporting drama, should finally be intertwined. Britain's greatest playwright deserves his place not only at the heart of the Opening Ceremony, but also at the centre of the London 2012 Festival. If 'all the world's a stage' then William Shakespeare took a starring role, showcasing Britain around the globe at London 2012.

Film director Danny Boyle, best known for the Oscar-winning *Slumdog Millionaire* and the iconic *Trainspotting*, chose the 'Isles of Wonder' theme for the Opening Ceremony because he believed it captured the essence of Britain. 'Caliban's speech, which is one of the most beautiful speeches in Shakespeare, is about the wondrous beauty of the island and in this case Caliban's deep, personal devotion and affection for it,' he said. 'That was something we all felt going into the show and wanted to reflect. We wanted to celebrate the whole of the country … there are so many Isles of Wonder.'

It was also appropriate that St George's Day, the anniversary of Shakespeare's birth and death and a date that remembers England's patron saint, marked the launch of the World Shakespeare Festival on 23 April 2012. Unprecedented in scope and ambition, it formed the heart of the London 2012 Festival and marked the culmination of the Cultural Olympiad, the arts programme for the Games. Its aim was to bring the biggest audiences to the biggest Shakespeare celebration that the world has ever seen.

The plan was to showcase as many international artists as possible, in tribute to the 204 nations taking part in the sporting programme of the Games. Both sports and plays have a true global presence, with many famous sports originating in Britain and adopted with enthusiasm by the rest of the world. Similarly no other playwright has exercised such universal appeal as Shakespeare; half the schoolchildren in the world will encounter his work. Written in the reigns of Elizabeth I and her successor James I, his many plays and sonnets have endured more than four centuries to another Queen Elizabeth's reign, addressing such powerful themes as love, power, jealousy, death, war and revenge.

The impact of the World Shakespeare Festival resounded from Stratford-upon-Avon to almost every corner of the British Isles of Wonder, including Scotland, Northern Ireland and Wales. The 70 productions on show ranged from the experimental to the classic, the left-field to the grand. They were staged in venues big and small, among them the Barbican and the Royal Opera House. High-profile productions included *Timon of Athens* with Simon Russell Beale at the National Theatre and Jonathan Pryce as *King Lear* at the Almeida. A short film depicting Russell Beale and Olympic and Paralympic athletes, including Sydney 2000 Triple Jump champion and world record holder Jonathan Edwards reciting Caliban's lines from *The Tempest*, was produced to promote the Festival and reiterate the link between sporting and cultural themes. 'It's clear,' said Edwards 'that artists, just as athletes, are looking to make the best work of their lives this summer with the eyes of the world on the UK.' In the same way that elite names in sport can encourage the fun-runners and the Sunday morning rowers, the rallying call also inspired 7,200 performers from 260 amateur groups to perform in pubs, parks, castles and churches, encouraging a new wave of creativity.

Even as the Olympic Park was built in a neglected part of east London, the Globe Theatre that Shakespeare knew stood beyond the city walls in then disreputable, run-down Southwark. In 2012 the reconstructed Globe Theatre staged 37 of his plays performed in as many languages. *Richard III*, his compelling dissection of power and paranoia, was performed in Mandarin by the National Theatre of China; Theatre Wallay from Lahore presented The *Taming of the Shrew*, exploring the difficulties encountered by modern Pakistani women; the Habima National Theatre from Tel Aviv boldly tackled the humiliation of Shylock in *The Merchant of Venice*; and the Globe's own company put on *Henry V*, inviting the audience on a voyage of imagination with its powerful opening cry of 'O, for a Muse of fire'.

The British Museum mounted its own blockbuster exhibition called *Shakespeare: Staging the World*, offering historical insights into the capital that staged his plays. Huge crowds of around 3,000 would come to watch performances at the Globe, braving a neighbourhood frequented by prostitutes, pickpockets and other unsavoury characters. Even society's elite came to sit in the Globe's balconies on the 'wrong' side of the Thames. In fact the theatre admitted anyone, from barons to beggars, shoemakers to servant girls, as long as he or she had a coin of the realm to drop in a box before entering.

The Royal Shakespeare Company (RSC), the umbrella producer of the World Shakespeare Festival, commissioned 12 new productions, all of which premiered in Stratford-upon-Avon. A version of *Much Ado About Nothing* opened at The Courtyard Theatre, for example, before transferring to London's West End. Set in India, it marked the RSC debut of actress Meera Syal, who played Beatrice. The Wooster Group from New York City incorporated ground-breaking multimedia into its co-production of *Troilus and Cressida*, the epic Trojan play about war, love and politics.

Deborah Shaw, associate director of the RSC and director of the World Shakespeare Festival, was charged with the task of presenting the playwright in a whole new light to diverse audiences, many seeing his work for the first time. 'So many people know Britain through its culture and literature and we wanted to put that on show, but also invite our international peers to join in,' she explained. The Festival assembled world-class actors, artists and directors to celebrate the stories, characters, relationships and language of Shakespeare that is etched into all of us and has helped nations, new and old, to define themselves. If you've ever been 'more sinned against than sinning', you're quoting Shakespeare. If you think it's 'high time' to deal with something in 'one fell swoop', you're quoting Shakespeare, so great his influence on the English language. Notably in an Olympic and Paralympic year, his work mentions nearly 50 sports and games, many of which were played out in the other Stratford during the summer of 2012. Wrestling appears in *As You Like It*, football in *King Lear* and *The Comedy of Errors* and fencing in *Hamlet*. Archery features in *A Midsummer Night's Dream*, *King Lear* and *The Taming of the Shrew*, and tennis in *All's Well That Ends Well*, *Henry V* and *Pericles*.

Shaw has been staging regional and national Shakespeare festivals for years, from the Bath Shakespeare Festival to the RSC's Complete Works. Her own journeys of imagination have involved trawling the world for weird and wonderful interpretations, from physical theatre to circuses, from Bremen and Baghdad to Brazil. As a schoolgirl living down the road from Stratford-upon-Avon, she was first gripped by Shakespeare when an English teacher took her to see RSC productions. Now she lives in a cottage next to the farm once owned by Shakespeare's grandfather. Shaw is married to Iraqi theatre director Monadhil Daood, whom she met while scouting for interesting international productions. He brought a production called *Romeo and Juliet in Baghdad* to the UK for the World Shakespeare Festival, which received great audience acclaim.

The Festival was four years in the planning after first being included in the original bid to host the London 2012 Games. The RSC went around the world to look for interesting theatre. The Arab Spring attracted their attention, leading to a commissioned piece from Tunisia. With Rio hosting the 2016 Games, they decided to embark on two projects with Brazilian companies. 'Different countries shed different light on Shakespeare,' Shaw noted. 'The similarities to theatre with sport are also quite interesting in an Olympic and Paralympic year. You've got your theatre company, your manager, your cast and your rehearsal process, a bit like the coach, the team and the training. My role is to give people great Shakespeare and inspire them in the same way that I was inspired. Each generation has to discover the work for themselves and it's our job to put great theatre in front of them in all different forms – whether it is Brazilians doing acrobatics, Iraqis doing Romeo and Juliet with a character wearing a Lionel Messi shirt or a full-blown Julius Caesar.'

Shaw's mission was for the Festival to inspire her audiences with a lifelong love of Shakespeare's work and a recognition of how it can speak directly to them. His plays were hugely popular with ordinary people as well as courtiers, providing compelling entertainment in an age when only eight per cent of the population could read. 'He was walking the line between thieves, robbers, vagabonds and actors, but with an ear to the people who pulled the levers of power,' she observed. 'He was in the Court and on the street. The kind of energy in his plays is anarchic. Shakespeare has a place at the top table of art, but actually he was writing for the people. And he knew who they were.' Such perception has allowed his work to endure, speaking to new generations across the world as powerfully as to his English contemporaries. Michael Boyd, Artistic Director of the RSC, has described Shakespeare as 'the favourite playwright of the whole world', adding, 'People of all races, creeds and continents have chosen to gather around his work to share stories of what it is like to be human. To fall in love or fall from grace.' The World Shakespeare Festival acknowledges the extraordinary achievement of this most international of artists even as London welcomes the world to celebrate the Olympic and Paralympic Games.

A Festival of Hope and Glory

Sarah Edworthy

A feast of cultural inspiration from the London 2012 Festival delights audiences across the UK

At 10.15pm on 8 September 2012, in a nicely judged cameo on stage at the Royal Albert Hall, the finale to the 118th season of Britain's famous Henry Wood Promenade Concerts moved into another realm. The spectacle cross-fertilised art with sport and placed Olympic and Paralympic action in a cultural context, thrilling vast crowds watching on giant screens in Hyde Park, City Hall in Glasgow, the Owain Glundwr Playing Fields in Caerphilly and Belfast's Titanic Slipways.

The Last Night of the Proms is by a long, fervent and quintessentially British tradition the world's biggest and least self-conscious celebration of classical music. In the year when the capital hosted the Olympic Games for the third time, the BBC Proms season became a cornerstone of the London 2012 Festival – the 12-week extravaganza of live performance and art staged across the United Kingdom to complement the Games. The Proms featured the world's leading artists such as Daniel Barenboim, who conducted his West-Eastern Divan orchestra in a complete Beethoven Symphony cycle, as well as the largest number of new commissions for a Proms season, record youth participation and a focus upon London itself. The annual 'Last Night' show of patriotism was timed to coincide with the penultimate night of Games action, providing a fitting hurrah for an incredible British summer of sport, celebration and display.

The evening unfolded in a skilful blend of tradition and surprise. Conductor Jiří Bělohlávek, making a valedictory appearance with the BBC Symphony Orchestra, had led violinist Nicola Benedetti, tenor Joseph Calleja and his orchestra through a programme of operatic arias by Verdi, Massenet and Puccini, the universally loved Bruch Violin Concerto and a choral work by Delius. It had reached the point where the Prommers threaten to take over, swaying and swirling flags to an emotional *Land of Hope and Glory*. Then Calleja returned on stage, dressed in a Team GB tracksuit, to lead the traditional roof-raising *Rule Britannia*. After a magnificent rendition Bělohlávek playfully suggested another 'with some help'. To tumultuous applause, gold and silver medallists from the Team GB and ParalympicsGB Rowing squads strode on to the stage, medals round their necks and Union flags round their shoulders, ready to lend their support. The night ended with the BBC Symphony Chorus performing a synchronised 'Mobot' in tribute to track champion Mo Farah as the singers took their applause following one last chorus of *Rule Britannia*.

It was a symbolic unifying moment, vividly described by George Hall in the *Guardian*. 'A stroke of genius was the evening's emotional and visual climax – bringing on to the platform gold and silver medal-winning members of Team GB and ParalympicsGB as part of the patriotic bonanza that forms the traditional grand finale; all that was missing was for the Queen to abseil down from the gallery and lead the singing of *Rule, Britannia!* herself. Maybe next year,' he observed.

If calls to 'keep the Flame alive' after the success of the Olympic and Paralympic Games have focused on encouraging more people to play competitive sport, this glorious medley of music and medals confirmed that the cultural flame has also been well nourished by London 2012.

The 12-week finale brought to a fascinating climax the four-year programme of artistic events that had begun at the end of the Beijing 2008 Games. This innovative programme brought together the government, the Mayor's office, the BBC, the Arts Council and many other stakeholders to create an enduring artistic legacy and encourage future tourists to come to Great Britain. For every world-class athlete that inspired awe and applause in the Olympic Stadium, there have been world-class artists to appreciate: David Hockney, Barenboim, Pina Bausch, Danny Boyle, Thomas Heatherwick and Damien Hirst, to name but a few.

Many of the programme's highlights were inspired by the symbols of the Olympic Games. Almost three million people helped perform Martin Creed's massive interactive performance art project, Work No. 1197, by ringing bells of all shapes and sizes – church bells, bike bells, door bells and a ringing-bell app downloaded to smartphones – at 8.12am on 27 July, the day the Olympic Games opened. Other highlights took their lead from the symbolism of the Olympic Flame, from the stunning fire garden installed at Stonehenge by Compagnie Carabosse to the pyrotechnic display on Lake Windermere and the 'Connecting Light' installation along the 2,000-year-old, 73-mile length of Hadrian's Wall.

The breathtaking athletic achievements of Jessica Ennis,

Usain Bolt, Beth Tweddle, David Weir, Ellie Simmonds and so many others were given an artistic parallel in the extraordinary performance by Elizabeth Streb. The daredevil American choreographer blends circus skills, dance and gymnastics in her work, as she and her team abseiled down City Hall and the London Eye in an act entitled 'One Extraordinary Day'. The mass arrival of the world's elite athletes in the Olympic Village was reflected in the numbers participating together in Big Dance 2012, an eight-day show of community dance involving hundreds of thousands of people across the UK, from Trafalgar Square to local shopping centres, public parks to schools. Everywhere you could see reflected the theme of International Respect – memorably in the fabulous BT River of Music weekend of free concerts along the Thames. Here a typical collaboration was that between Welsh folk group 9Bach and the indigenous Australian musicians who comprise The Black Arm Band Company. They spearheaded a project called 'Mamiaith – Mother Tongue', focusing on the preservation of language and culture through music and song.

The numbers that drove the London 2012 Festival were Olympic in scale. More than 25,000 artists from all competing nations contributed their talents. More than 10 million free tickets were available for 12,000 events at 900 venues spanning the length and breadth of Britain, including 130 world premieres and 85 premieres in the UK. By the end of August 2012 more than 19.5 million people had joined in the celebrations, while 16.5 million free opportunities had drawn in new audiences.

Arts festivals have been a component of the Olympic Games since ancient Greek times. To mark London 2012 the United Nations called for a worldwide laying-down of arms during the Games, and the truce ideal inspired many of the boldest Festival events. 'Peace Camp', for example, was an incredibly beautiful, quixotic vision. Directed by theatre and opera director Deborah Warner, working in collaboration with actress Fiona Shaw, composer Mel Mercier and sound artist John Del'Nero, it consisted of an audio-visual installation staged in seven far-flung rural coastal sites around Britain and Northern Ireland. Small sealed tents shone through the night over cliffs and sea below, subtly shifting the colour of their glow from white to pink to yellow and back again.'There are no fixed paths to follow,' explained Rupert Christiansen in the *Daily Telegraph*, 'but as you wander freely through the encampment, you will hear – as if it was hanging in the air – a soundscape of love poetry embedded in a tapestry of words, signals and noises which will play in counterpoint to the ambient roars and whispers of the wind and waves. On the eve of the Olympic Games, the tents offer from the sea a beacon of welcome to our shores.'

The glowing fairy-tale environment conjured by French arts group Compagnie Carabosse in 'The Fire Garden' at Stonehenge – flaming fire pots, cascades of candles, fire sculptures and so on – inspired visitors to the timeless stone circles with the Olympic and Paralympic spirit. Hadrian's Wall, the 2,000-year-old boundary stretching from Wallsend to Bowness-on-Solway, was illuminated by 450 giant balloons fitted with LED lights, pulsating in different colours along its length. 'We are imagining a reverse wall – an inverse of the border. The border was built to separate people, and we want to bring them together again,' revealed Zachary Lieberman of the New York-based digital arts collective YesYesNo. Barenboim's well-received Beethoven cycle was played by the West-Eastern Divan Orchestra he formed with Edward Said in 1999, composed of musicians from Israel, Palestine and other Arab countries. 'Countries where the open ear has been too often replaced by the unsheathed sword, to the detriment of all,' said the Israeli pianist and conductor, who was born in Argentina.

Rather than a Best of British theme, the Festival celebrated international collaboration to an extraordinary degree. 'We're going way past the world of flags,' said theatre director Peter Sellars, director of the 1990 and 1993 Los Angeles Festivals, cultural extravaganzas inspired by the 1984 LA Games. Sellars' contribution to London 2012 brought together American novelist Toni Morrison and Malian singer Rokia Traore in a re-imagining of the relationship between Shakespeare's Desdemona and her African nurse, performed at the Barbican. The Shakespeare Festival, which presented 37 productions by companies from 37 countries, celebrated the poet's famous description of all the world as a stage. And of the 100,000 people who attended, 80,000 were first-timers – a valuable statistic for those seeking to engage with future audiences. In Birmingham 'The Voyage' celebrated the city's heritage of cultural migration in a show featuring song, dance and aerial acrobatics. It was staged by the Sydney-based physical theatre company Legs on the Wall, whose director Patrick Nolan enthused, 'One of the things that becomes very apparent when you're in Birmingham is the extraordinary mix of cultures that live in the city … we felt that was a lovely echo of the Olympic Games and the spirit of the Games.'

Good art opens eyes, provokes thought and invites contemplation, but that literal sense of introduction, of opening up new worlds, was perhaps seen nowhere more poignantly than in the freezing rain one night near Stirling Castle. Here Gustavo Dudamel's Simon Bolivar Orchestra, composed of young people from shanty towns in Venezuela, played alongside youngsters from the Raploch estate, where music is transforming lives. The children are members of Sistema Scotland, a radical social-intervention programme based on the model that produced the Venezuelan musicians and changed the lives of children of an underprivileged community through immersion in classical music. 'What can you do creatively that is once in a lifetime? I think Gustavo Dudamel and Simon Bolivar turning up in Raploch is once in a lifetime,' said Ruth Mackenzie, revealing the pressure to stage events whose impact will endure into the future. 'I'll never forget the faces [in Raploch],' wrote Tony Hall, Chair of the Cultural Olympiad Board, in the *Daily Telegraph*. 'Nor will I forget the buzz round the Paul Hamlyn Hall at the Royal Opera House when homeless people came to perform – the first time ever in an Olympic festival. Or the excitement in the faces of the young people from East London, out of work for more than six months, but now on work placements to festival projects as part of our creative jobs scheme. We can't lose all this.'

And we won't, according to Peter Sellars, reflecting on the impact of the Los Angeles Arts Festival of 1984. He believes the London 2012 Festival, and the Games themselves, will have a catalytic effect on the capital and the nation; the cultural flame will continue to burn. 'It woke people up to LA as a cultural site and we were able to follow through on that in the 1990s and explore the city as a cultural destination. The LA Arts Festival re-drew people's internal maps, and [The London 2012 Festival] will almost certainly do that for London, too.'

The long list of colourful, exciting, weird and wonderful cultural offerings from the London 2012 Festival has left poignant and joyful memories across the UK. Momentum is established, with audiences determine to see and embrace more events in future. There is a growing appetite to feed, an excitement to foster, as Hall notes. 'When thinking about future activities, we need to hold on to the key principles that have guided this cultural festival and made it such a success – world-class art and artists, celebrating and reflecting diversity, rooted in communities and involving everyone. Watch this space,' he promises.

'I wanted everyone to be part of it ... I saw for myself the collective pull of the Olympic Flame and all it symbolises.'

Ben Ainslie, four-time Olympic gold medallist and the first Torchbearer of the Olympic Torch Relay

3

THE LONDON 2012 TORCH RELAYS

Great Britain's Moment to Shine

Great Britain's Moment to Shine

Sarah Edworthy

In the wettest summer for decades, the Olympic and Paralympic Torch Relays kindled excitement, inspiration and hope across Great Britain

On 27 July the Opening Ceremony of the Olympic Games dazzled audiences around the world with its spectacle and imagination. The most memorable moment for many came in the dramatic conclusion, as the iconic Cauldron was lit to symbolise the start of the Games. These last minutes of a compelling three hours were full of surprise and delight. Sir Steve Redgrave, then Great Britain's greatest Olympian, brought the Flame into the Olympic Stadium, then unveiled the 'real' final Torchbearers – seven young British athletes nominated by seven British Olympic heroes. In an inspiring finale the teenagers lit seven of the copper petals carried into the Stadium by each competing nation. As tongues of fire spread from one to another, the petals rose up and converged into a Cauldron in a beautiful and powerfully moving display.

This glorious moment celebrated both an end and a beginning. For the opening of the Olympic Games also marked the end of the 70-day Torch Relay – an epic, magnificent journey that had stoked anticipation for the Games right across the UK. From the day that the

Olympic Flame arrived on British soil, at 7.24 pm on Friday 18 May, it captured the nation's imagination. When the gold-liveried A319, listed as flight BA2012 and called 'The Firefly', approached to land at Royal Naval Air Station Culdrose in Cornwall, the emotional charge of the occasion took spectators by surprise. The tiny spark inside a golden ceremonial lantern, carried with pride by HRH The Princess Royal and welcomed by a party including Lord Coe, Deputy Prime Minister Nick Clegg, senior representatives of the Armed Forces, and David Beckham, suddenly took on huge significance. As the Princess Royal observed, 'It's only when the Flame comes into your possession and actually gets here, that you really realise, this is it.'

The Olympic Torch Relay began at Land's End in Cornwall and travelled 8,000 miles, with 8,000 Torchbearers forming a human chain. Ben Ainslie, who had been given the honour of being the first Torchbearer, recalls the reaction which 'blew him away' when he set off from under the iconic signpost at Land's End. 'At 7.08 am, when my Torch was pumping out a big Flame in the breeze, cameras clicked, people cheered, clapped and whistled,' he recalled. 'I didn't have any particular plan of action, I didn't know how fast I should run, but everyone was so excited I decided to walk. I wanted everyone to be part of it. People stretched hands out to touch the Torch; they held up babies to get a better glimpse of the Flame ... I saw for myself the collective pull of the Olympic Flame and all it symbolises.'

The Flame's journey revealed many regions of natural beauty, from rivers and mountains to rolling farmland, isolated islands to beaches and moors. It also visited a wide range of castles, cathedrals, stately homes, towers, bridges, water wheels, sculpture parks and bustling, modern city centres. Crowds gathered to welcome the Flame to St Michael's Mount in Cornwall, the Giant's Causeway in Northern Ireland and the Regency elegance of Bath's Royal Crescent. The Torch Relay made dawn visits to the mysterious stone circles of Callanish on the Isle of Lewis and Stonehenge in Wiltshire, and enjoyed lively evening events across the country, with the Flame resting in a Celebration Cauldron lit by the last Torchbearer of the day. Durdle Door on Dorset's Jurassic Coast reflected the power of nature, while visits to Iron Bridge in Shropshire or at the Laxey Wheel on the Isle of Man paid tribute to the country's entrepreneurial tradition. A perfect showcase for Great Britain's landscape and history, the Torch Relay will inspire many new visitors to explore both the country and its artistic hinterland.

Mostly, however, the Torch Relay was a celebration of people. An unquenchable human spirit combined with the sense of history being made as the Olympic Flame touched ordinary residential streets and town centres, an enduring echo of a glorious summer. The stories behind the nominated Torchbearers, almost half of whom were aged between 12 and 24, often revealed courageous people who had overcome all manner of illness, made light of disability or survived personal tragedy. They flourished in the spotlight of appreciation and respect, displaying a compelling joie de vivre along their 300m stretches.

As Torchbearers took their turn to walk, run, dance, skip, do a jig, travel by wheelchair and even perform acrobatics, they built up a groundswell of expectation and delight that contributed to the special atmosphere of the London 2012 Games. Several former servicemen and women were among them, offering remarkable displays of tenacity and courage. Enthusiasm and respect spun outwards like a ripple. Tentative comments on social media such as 'Eating my words here, but this is truly special, right?' quickly evolved into a chorus of ecstatic cheers from crowded roadsides, jubilant patriotic street parties and a nationwide addiction to following the minute-by-minute action online via BBC's Torchcam.

Both the Olympic and Paralympic Torches shared the same core design but featured different finishes – a complementary echo, like the Sun and Moon. The Olympic Torch was covered in sparkling gold to capture the celebratory spirit of the occasion, while the Paralympic Torch had a mirror finish to stand out as a gleaming beacon during its journey through the night. Edward Barber and Jay Osgerby won the opportunity to design the Torch following a competitive tender run by LOCOG and the Design Council. The challenge was technical as well as aesthetic, recalled Osgerby. 'The Torch had to operate across a certain temperature range (-10 to +40 degrees C), in winds gusting up to 75mph, at an altitude of 6,000 feet above sea level with a constant flame height and luminosity.' With only 10 days to produce a viable design, they worked through the night. 'From the moment we watched the announcement of London's winning bid, we were absolutely determined to win,' Osgerby explained.

The three-sided form of Barber Osgerby's winning design was perforated with 8,000 circles representing the stories of the 8,000 Torchbearers who were to carry the Flame on its 8,000-mile journey. The triangular shape was inspired by the trinities that recurred in the brief: the three Olympic Values of respect, excellence and friendship; the three elements of the Olympic motto 'Faster, Higher, Stronger'; the fact that London would become Host City for the third time in 2012, following the 1908 and 1948 Games; and the legacy aims in business, sport and education. In the hands of each Torchbearer, the majority 'ordinary' people nominated by others for their extraordinary inspirational qualities, the Torch became a powerful beacon of inspiration and hope.

The Paralympic Torch Relay took a different format, one that paid proud tribute to the Paralympic movement's homegrown origins. On top of the highest peaks in the four Home Nations – Slieve Donard in Northern Ireland, Snowdon in Wales, Ben Nevis in Scotland and Scafell Pike in England's Lake District - four Paralympic Flames were kindled. Four teams, made up of Scouts, mountain guides and people with disabilities, scaled the high peaks, bringing each Flame down again in ceremonial miners' lanterns. Scout leader Richard Dorrian, who was at the top of Slieve Donard, described the complexity of the task. 'The weather was a wee bit misty which made it a bit tricky lighting the actual fire. We were not allowed to use natural fire-lighting equipment like matches so had to use dry grass and kindling. After a few attempts it ignited into the places it was supposed to ignite,' he explained.

That same spirit of endeavour and teamwork was replicated on Scafell and Ben Nevis, and on Snowdon, where Lord Coe joined the trek to the summit. Elaine Peart, who has bipolar disorder, became the first person to carry the Flame there. 'I was chosen as a representative of a group I am a member of, as other people are not able physically to take part. It was absolutely incredible and amazing. I hope it will help people realise that people do have more to offer, and that a disability needn't set you back. I am looking forward to the Games even more now, and I feel I have contributed a tiny atom towards it,' she revealed.

The four Paralympic Flames became the focus of festivities in London, Cardiff, Edinburgh and Belfast over the

August Bank Holiday weekend before coming together in Stoke Mandeville. Here they united in a Cauldron to form one symbolic Paralympic Flame. Eva Loeffler, daughter of the founder of the Paralympic Games, Dr Ludwig Guttmann, addressed the crowds before the Flame-lighting Ceremony, paying tribute to the role played by the Stoke Mandeville Games in defining the modern Paralympic Movement. The theme for the Paralympic Torch Relay was 'Light the Way', and the scene was set by a lantern procession of 150 local residents. They formed a guard of honour for the eight Torchbearers who had carried the Flames as representatives of the four Home Nations.

At 8pm on 28 August the Paralympic Flame embarked on its 92-mile journey to the Olympic Stadium in Stratford. The 24-hour Relay featured 580 Torchbearers, working in 116 teams of five. Each individual was selected for how their life stories demonstrated the Paralympic Values of courage, determination, inspiration and equality; each collective symbolised the unifying power of sport and team camaraderie. Young and old, they included Sally Haynes, who competed in the first Paralympic Games at Rome 1960 and went on to compete at a further three Games in the Epée event of Wheelchair Fencing.

The Relay travelled through cheering tunnels of noise and applause in Buckinghamshire, Hertfordshire and all six of the London's Host Boroughs to the Olympic Stadium. Like its Olympic counterpart, the Paralympic Torch Relay stopped to share the historic moment and to pose for enduring photographic images at iconic locations – notably in Maida Vale, where the Flame was carried over the Abbey Road zebra crossing made famous by the Beatles album cover, in London Zoo in Regent's Park, where it was held aloft in the penguin enclosure, and in

Brent, where the Torch was taken up the steps to Britain's first traditional Hindu temple, the Shri Swaminarayan Mandir temple.

Dame Tanni Grey-Thompson, Paralympic swimmer Chris Holmes and former boxer Michael Watson were in the team that proceeded along Regent Street and through Piccadilly Circus. Watson, left paralysed after a boxing match in 1991, had been told he would never walk again. Through sheer grit he managed his first steps in 1997, and in 2003 completed the London Marathon over six days. He, like so many exemplary people who formed the London 2012 Olympic and Paralympic Torch Relays, summed up the thrill of spreading a powerful sense of optimism. 'I am over the moon and just very, very proud to have been selected to carry the Flame,' he said.

On 9 September 2012 the Paralympic Games came to an end, commemorated in a spectacular conflagration of special fire effects, 'The Festival of the Flame'. The Closing Ceremony, led by Coldplay, Jay Z and Rihanna in a vivid flame-orange dress, saw the Flame in the Olympic Cauldron ceremonially extinguished. And a whole country that had fallen in love with its glorious summer of sport paused to reflect on what had been achieved. For the feelgood factor of London 2012, symbolised by the living Olympic and Paralympic Flames, went beyond a relish of sporting success. In embracing the spirit of celebration, support and respect for others that lies at the heart of the Olympic and Paralympic Games, the nation has changed, and grown. Keeping this spirit alive, not least through memories of two magnificent Torch Relays, will be one of the proudest legacies of London 2012.

'We wanted to bring athletes and spectators closer than ever before, to re-establish the chemistry and magic between athlete and crowd.'

Kevin Owens

4

DAWN OF THE GAMES

6.30am Day One: 28 July 2012

'Isles of Wonder' Welcome the Games

6.30am Day One: 28 July 2012

Kevin Owens

*The glorious Olympic Park, six years in the making,
welcomes the world to its inspiring landscape, venues
and atmosphere*

For the past six years my eye has always been on the clock.
Watching the calendar, counting down the days. A series of
markers that were noted and celebrated. 2012 days to go,
5 years to go, 4 years to go, 3 years, 1,000 days, 2 years, 500
days, 1 year, 100 days, 2012 hours … The date that has
been in my diary for my whole time as Design Principal for
the London Organising Committee of the Olympic Games
and Paralympic Games has finally arrived. My life through
a countdown clock is complete. We are here. It is now.

Walking through the Olympic Park in the early morning light on this day as the gates are about to open is
a slightly surreal moment. My mind is buzzing with numbers. Five kilometres of riverbanks have been cleaned up
and 35 bridges built. Two million tonnes of contaminated
soil has been washed and an incredible 6,200 new trees,
9,500 shrubs, 63,000 bulbs, 250,000 wetlands plants
and 766,000 grasses and ferns have been planted. There
are 148,000 seats to be occupied, 10,500 athletes, 204
competing nations and 302 medal ceremonies. This place
has transformed. It is hard to even begin to remember

what was here before – six years feels like a lifetime. From centuries of dereliction and neglect to this… The smell of fresh-cut grass, the tranquil water, the beautifully manicured gardens and the burst of glorious colour from the wildflower meadows. The stage is set, our venues are pristine, the Park is complete. Holding our collective breath in anticipation, we are on our marks and ready for the 30th Olympiad.

Last night, steeped in history, we launched our very British Games with a bang. The Opening Ceremony captured the essence of our team's aspirations and set the scene for an Olympic Games that celebrates the nation's colourful past while embracing the inspiration of future generations. This Games will revel in the very best of British – slightly eccentric, full of humour, but always presented with pride. The surprise and delight delivered through the Opening Ceremony now has the ability to be translated throughout the Games – although unlikely to include Her Majesty The Queen and James Bond again! Today we open our doors to the world to celebrate our future in the biggest new park for over a hundred years.

Just above me on the main Stratford bridge, I can hear the distant strains of the Royal Marines band playing John Williams' *Olympic Fanfare*. The moment is poignant, the gates are open. There is a buzz of excitement from those lucky spectators with their prized tickets in hand: they too have dreamed of this moment for many months. This is their moment. The Games have truly begun. Within hours medals will be won, hearts broken and dreams realised, all in a part of this amazing city that was once forgotten and lost. Working on the Olympic and Paralympic Games, I always thought I understood the power of these events, but it is only during the last 12 hours that it has been driven home – the realisation of the incredible feat to bring together people from every country in the world, all with the same goal of achieving excellence. All happening in a place that we have created. It is a life-changing moment.

The Park sits at the south of the Lee Valley Regional Park, a sprawling green ribbon that connects leafy Hertfordshire to the north with the bustle of the Thames. Although it is easy to romanticise the chequered history of this part of east London, it was an arterial block in the city, culminating in a poisoned, post-industrial wasteland. Standing beneath the twisted forms of The Orbit, I try to visualise the Great Eastern Railway works, a derelict collection of rail heads and sheds, to which this was once home. It severed the local communities, compounded by the surrounding deep railway sidings, contaminated rivers and canals, and arterial roads. By the time we commenced the works in 2006, the site was an unregulated resultant mix of piles of fridges, breakers' yards, abandoned cars and derelict warehouses. We knew the potential of the site would provide us with our greatest challenge, intertwined as it was with railways, roads and, most importantly, rivers. And the water was also our greatest asset, once lost within the post-industrial landscape. We had to seize the opportunity to reinvigorate the waterways, reveal them and establish a new parkland setting.

Rather than being delivered as a traditional sporting event, in London we wanted to deliver the magic of the Olympic and Paralympic Games in a Park that truly reflected their festival nature – a relaxed, informal setting that would redefine what it means to be a part of the Games. An open, inclusive space that would embrace London's moment, and be worthy of this once-in-a-lifetime opportunity to celebrate Great Britain on a global stage.

The Olympic Park builds on the rich heritage of London's Royal Parks to deliver an exceptional Park for the 21st century. The rivers and green lawns at its core are pivotal to the spectators' Olympic and Paralympic experience – London's Olympic Park has been designed truly as a Park, and not a pedestrian concourse. Pathways meander along river edges, through the rushes and reeds, leading to the woodland settings and the rolling lawns of the wetlands bowl and ParkLive. Together they anchor the venues and sporting experience in a unique Olympic setting like never before. The Park is at the heart of our Games.

Our success will ultimately be measured by those who experience our Games directly. Judging by the smiles on the faces on the bridge above me, we're off to a good start! Reassuringly Dr Jacques Rogge, President of the International Olympic Committee (IOC), approved of the result. He was quoted, 'In the Olympic Park one senses that the collective excitement and anticipation of tens of thousands of sports fans has been captured and magnified into one spirit. There are just enough people to build the atmosphere, but not too many to spoil the experience. There are huge areas collectively to enjoy the sport, but small corners for some rest and relaxation. Amazing vision added to attention to detail; like so much created here, it's a triumph.' Words for us all to celebrate.

The crowds are now building, and their excitement is being transferred to the venues themselves. I hear the cheers from within the belly of the Aquatics Centre; the sound of anticipation pervades the air. Both the Park and the venues are bursting into life. It's inspiring to think that within these venues over the coming days we will crown over 300 new Olympic champions, and hopefully set the dreams in place for future generations.

As a design team, we always knew from the outset that we wanted to create an environment like no other for the Olympic and Paralympic Games. Our brief was to design a Games for the people – a place to share, a stage for a festival. The Park sets the scene for our celebration, and the venues continue the theme right through to the competition fields of play. We wanted to bring athletes and spectators closer than ever before, to re-establish the chemistry and magic between athlete and crowd. We were fortunate enough to be able to consult with the best of Team GB, taking their advice on what makes the ultimate arena for sporting excellence. Whether it be Sir Chris Hoy cycling round a velodrome or Jonathan Edwards leaping within a stadium, the message was clear – the crowd makes the difference. All our venues attempt to reinforce this message, and to create the most intimate and atmospheric sporting arenas. Watching sport at the London 2012 Games was designed to be a participatory experience, with the crowd up close to the action – an active, flag-waving, cheering role to be played by everyone.

The flags of the world are indeed out today – not only for Day One of the Olympic Games, but also for our very special guests. This morning I have the honour of being in the party greeting the Queen and Prince Philip at the top of The Orbit. This is most definitely not your average day… Shooting up to the heady heights in the lift, I reflect that six years ago that I would have never thought I would be here on Day One: 22 storeys above the future Queen Elizabeth II Olympic Park, in the presence of the Queen herself. It was a wonderfully relaxed atmosphere. Her Majesty enthused about the beautiful colourful meadows below us, ultimately sharing her delight and pride in all that had been achieved in bringing the Games and Park to fruition. This made for an incredibly special moment on the most special of days.

This unique project has brought together some of the best creative talents across the UK. All aspects of design have been covered, whether it be civil engineering or graphics, architecture or landscape. The bringing together of permanent and temporary, legacy and festival has culminated in a richly diverse mix of offers within this new emerging landscape. For example, in the north of the Park there are two scales at play, the heroic and the whimsical. The anchor is provided by the sinuous timber form of Hopkins' Velodrome, set against the playful grand exterior of Wilkinson Eyre's Basketball Arena. Both structures are complemented by an array of lighter, more playful touches, including an inflatable bandstand, Peter Lewis' *Running Water* (waterfall bridge), the idiosyncratic *Walk in the Park* red telephone boxes and the playful narrative of Thomas Klassnik's *Fantasticology* facts peppered throughout the Park. Throughout we have sought to build upon our heritage, drawing upon our past, but with a singular vision delivering a confident and innovative celebration of our future.

The fact that over 30 years of development have been condensed into an intense six-year build period has forced us to collectively review what we wanted to achieve, and fundamentally how we were going to do it. There was no room for error, no room for ambiguity – this had to be right first time, sprinting out of the blocks for the shorter race of 2012, but prepared for the marathon of the years ahead. Sitting on the banks of the River Lea on this remarkable day, I can feel that we have truly fulfilled our promise. The team has delivered an Olympic Park like never before, and delivered it with a clear single vision that will resonate in the hearts and minds of all who experience it for years to come. We have shaped the legacy of an epic summer.

Although the joy of the Games has now arrived, paradoxically I am tinged with sadness. We are complete, the creative process has run its course, we are here. The Park, in its box-fresh state, will never be like this again – full of expectation, brimming with colour, ready. Our success will be measured over the coming weeks, but now we have done all we can. When we started on this journey we set our benchmarks high; we aspired to deliver the best we possibly could and to push beyond our own personal bests. Our inspiration was anchored by the steely determination of our athletes. We knew we had to do our part, and set the stage for the glories of sporting excellence. The stage is now set: over to you…

'Isles of Wonder' Welcome the Games

Tom Knight

Danny Boyle's stunning Olympic Games Opening Ceremony offers a British spectacle to dazzle the world

As 965 drummers, led by Dame Evelyn Glennie, beat out the pulsating rhythm of the industrial age, seven smoke-belching towering chimneys rose from England's green and pleasant land and Pandemonium reigned in the Olympic Stadium. The Opening Ceremony, now in its second element, was only nine minutes old. Yet I could not have been the only one watching who felt a shiver down the spine and was gripped by the realisation, 'This is good – seriously good'.

Within nine minutes we had already seen what the concept of London 2012 delivering a show 'differently' from Beijing 2008, once the subject of jokes, really meant. While most Opening Ceremonies I had seen began with a blank canvas, the 80,000-strong crowd making their way to their seats in the Olympic Stadium in Stratford looked out on green meadows, farmers tilling the soil, a village cricket match and maypole dancing. This was history's 'Isle of Wonder', a rural England from the 17th century. In the landscape, as promised by the artistic director Danny

Boyle, were real sheep, real horses, cows, goats, ducks, geese and even three sheepdogs to maintain some order.

Boyle also had something unique up his sleeve, courtesy of British technology: audience pixels. The 70,799 small panels of LEDs, controlled by a central computer, were attached to every seat. Linking the audience directly to the action, they produced a myriad complex images and beautiful effects throughout the Stadium.

Anyone who has seen a Danny Boyle-directed film will know how the man can grab the attention, make the viewer sit up in the seat, incite surprise, delight and a range of emotions with a sudden shift in tone. Remember *Slumdog Millionaire*? *Trainspotting*? Or even his early film, *Shallow Grave*? He also knows how to tug at the heartstrings, and, at the outset, the Opening Ceremony had the Boyle stamp writ large. Speaking ahead of the Ceremony, the Artistic Director explained: 'The job of an Opening Ceremony is to welcome the athletes to the city, so it's a kind of entertainment. It says "welcome, feel loved, feel warm, this is us".'

We began with a fast-moving montage of the River Thames' journey, travelling from its source in Kemble, Gloucestershire to the lights and skyscrapers of London and the new Olympic Park in Stratford. Images of Britain along the way included Ratty and Mole from Kenneth Grahame's *The Wind in the Willows*, the University Boat Race and Pink Floyd's flying pig over Battersea Power Station. Waving from afar were Olympians such as David Hemery, David Wilkie and Richard Mead. And within a few seconds, Boyle was up and running. The masterstroke was the appearance of Britain's newest sporting hero Bradley Wiggins, resplendent in his Yellow Jersey from victory in the Tour de France. He strode on stage in the Olympic

Stadium to ring the 23-ton Olympic Bell, the largest harmonically tuned bell in the world, made in east London by the Whitechapel Bell Company, founded in 1570.

The nationwide journey of the Olympic Flame via the Torch Relay was reflected in the specially commissioned filmed inserts of children's choirs singing their national songs in Wales, Northern Ireland and Scotland, while in the Olympic Stadium the Dockhead Choir sang *Jerusalem*. It was simple, emotional and very British – and we were only nine minutes in.

Then Boyle did it again. Sir Kenneth Branagh's arrival as the esteemed Victorian engineer Isambard Kingdom Brunel, all cigar-smoking, full of ingenuity and wittily followed by 50 more industrialists in top hats, heralded the change. Branagh's rendition of Caliban's speech from Shakespeare's *The Tempest* signalled the rise in tempo. 'Be not afeard,' he warned, surveying the green and pleasant land, 'the isle is full of noises.' And so it was.

The chimneys soared from the Stadium floor, ripping asunder everything that stood in their way. Before our eyes we saw England's green and pleasant land literally uprooted by the machines, factories and mills that fired the Industrial Revolution. The very people who worked at these factories were seen emerging from within the grassy hill at one end of the arena, just as they had poured from the countryside into the rapidly growing urban sprawls. This was not just an Opening Ceremony show: this was theatre. In the Olympic Stadium we saw the emergence of powerful cities such as Liverpool, Birmingham and Manchester. From these heartlands of trade and manufacture, the Industrial Revolution and all it set in train drove the growth of the British Empire and the transformation of individual lives. There was noise, smoke and a cast of thousands as the world that inspired novelists such as Dickens and Gaskell came vividly to life. Thundering drums accompanied Underworld's swirling *And I Will Kiss You* as 80,000 pairs of eyes in the Stadium struggled to take in the multitide of mini-dramas playing out below them.

This section of the Opening Ceremony was called *Pandemonium* – a name invented by the 17th-century poet John Milton in his epic poem *Paradise Lost*. Everything about *Pandemonium*, a name appropriately describing the capital city of Hell, evoked a 'different' Opening Ceremony, a glorious panoply of unexpected detail. There was a moment's stillness for the fallen of the First World War, and of all wars, in which the dead were represented by the names of the 'Accrington Pals' – men who famously lived, worked and died together in The Great War. We saw the industrial carnage give rise to the trades union movement, the Jarrow hunger march and the Suffragettes, whose numbers in the Olympic Stadium included Helen and Laura Pankhurst, great-granddaughter and great-great-granddaughter of Emily Pankhurst. A parade of figures from subsequent decades saw Pearly Kings and Queens interweave with the *Windrush* generation from the Caribbean and characters representing the Beatles and the so-called 'Swinging Sixties'.

So the crescendo of sound whirled on. Evelyn Glennie, barefoot to feel the rhythm of her playing better, drummed relentlessly on as the Olympic Stadium was bathed in striking blue light. Suddenly five giant glowing rings, forged in those industrial heartlands, were released into the night sky, still sparking from the furnaces below. In a spectacular climax the Olympic Rings rose and came together, the music stopped and the Olympic Stadium crowd applauded wildly.

Boyle had not finished playing the emotions of his

biggest-ever audience, however. As the cheering subsided, another filmed insert showed an innocuous black cab driving through the gates of Buckingham Palace. Its passenger emerges, but only when he reaches the top of the steps into the Palace do we see that it is Daniel Craig, aka James Bond. He is led into the Palace and, followed by three curious Corgis, Monty, Willow and Holly, into HM The Queen's private suite, where she is writing at a desk. She turns and – in a moment that had millions around the world wondering how London 2012 had managed it – says simply, 'Good evening, Mr Bond.'

Now Britain is known and revered for many things, but the Queen *acting* with fictional characters is not one of them. So this extraordinary Boyle twist reminded the world that, yes, we gave you the Industrial Revolution and everyone knows about our Royal Family, but we also gave you James Bond and life is better for it. This joke, though, was about to get even better.

The Queen and James Bond took to the air in an Augusta Westland AW 139 helicopter. It swept across London, through the arch of Tower Bridge and on to the Olympic Park. As the Stadium crowd heard the buzz of a helicopter overhead, the film showed the Queen put Bond aside to parachute first to the ground, all to the sound of the evocative James Bond theme, composed by Monty Norman in 1962. A magical moment for Her Majesty, celebrating her Diamond Jubilee. When she took her place in the Olympic Stadium, accompanied by the Duke of Edinburgh and Jacques Rogge, the President of the International Olympic Committee, wearing the same attire, the joke was complete.

No one would have even imagined the possibility of the Queen being party to the most exquisite joke, played to a worldwide audience of one billion people. Yet she chose to perform her first acting role in the Olympic Games Opening Ceremony, to great acclaim, even though the two skydivers were, in reality, Gary Connery (as the Queen) and Mark Sutton (James Bond). Yet for many the magnficent fiction is more powerful, and its memory will endure. Proof, if any were needed, that when it comes to ceremonies of any kind, the British can do the best.

And still more drama unfolded below. A moving and spectacular tribute to the National Health Service and Great Ormond Street Hospital saw 600 NHS staff dance around child patients, bouncing on 320 trampoline-sprung beds. In another unexpected move Mike Oldfield played along to the seminal *Tubular Bells*, the music that stayed in the charts for 279 weeks in the 1970s. The world's most successful author, JK Rowling, read from the opening paragraphs of JM Barrie's *Peter Pan* – the estate of which funds the Great Ormond Street Hospital – to launch Boyle's homage to Britain's great stable of children's literature. The audience was treated to an array of nightmarish villains. Captain Hook, Cruella de Vil and Voldemort were in turn banished from the Olympic Stadium by the arrival of 32 Mary Poppins, their carpet bags fluttering from the sky under their trusted umbrellas.

The arrival of Sir Simon Rattle and the London Symphony Orchestra appeared to bring a more serious tone, with a rendition of the Vangelis theme from the Oscar-winning film *Chariots of Fire*. Such an illusion was swiftly dispelled by the sight of Rowan Atkinson's silent comic creation Mr Bean, gloomily prodding the keys of the synthesiser. In what followed Mr Bean was both a bored and frustrated musician and, in a film-inserted dream sequence, a conniving athlete outwitting his hard-working teammates. Boyle wittily recreated the iconic *Chariots of Fire* scene in which Olympic athletes trained for the Paris 1924 Games by running along the sand at St Andrew's, Scotland. Thirty years before, at the 1981 Academy Awards, the film's screenwriter Colin Welland had announced, 'The British are coming'. In 2012, in the Olympic Stadium before an audience of millions, Boyle let it be known that the British had arrived, and were more than capable of laughing at themselves.

Some reviewers suggested that the Opening Ceremony had been a hotchpotch of ideas and themes, and that Boyle had thrown everything at it. There was truth in both comments, and the occasion was better for it. This was Boyle and London 2012 welcoming the world, and letting it in on some of our glorious and not-so-glorious national traits. His Ceremony was quirky, funny, emotional, very 'different' and quite brilliant in its pitch and presentation. Boyle admitted that he had accepted the job of directing the Ceremony as a tribute to his late father, who had ignited his own love of the Olympic Games when they watched grainy television pictures of the 1968 Mexico City Games. The emotion of those memories and of his father, whose birthday it would have been that day, was clearly apparent in Boyle's masterpiece in the Olympic Stadium.

The mood shifted again with the sporting hymn Abide With Me and a sequence entitled 'Frankie & June say... Thanks Tim', which played out the Saturday night out with a soundtrack of six decades, including David Bowie, The Who, Sex Pistols, The Clash and a live performance by Dizzee Rascal. The story of a young couple who meet through social networking ended with an appearance by Sir Tim Berners Lee, the inventor of the World Wide Web.

Everyone was here, it seemed, and that extended to

those chosen to carry the five-ringed Olympic flag into the Olympic Stadium. Dressed in white, the flagbearers included athlete Haile Gebrselassie, peace campaigner Leymah Gbowee, Doreen Lawrence, mother of the murdered Stephen Lawrence, Ban Ki-moon, the Secretary-General of the United Nations, and boxing legend Muhammad Ali, who had lit the Cauldron at the Atlanta 1996 Games. The 10,490 athletes from 204 countries entered the Olympic Stadium, led by famous and not-so-famous Flagbearers. Among those who received the biggest cheers were Usain Bolt, who carried the Jamaican flag, Maria Sharapova, who led the Russian Federation team, and Sir Chris Hoy, boldly brandishing the Union Jack at the head of Team GB – the final team to enter the Olympic Stadium. What puzzled many watching the parade of athletes was the presence alongside every Flagbearer of a child carrying what looked like a copper dish. Their role would become clear later in the evening.

In his speech of welcome, Jacques Rogge, President of the International Olympic Committee, told the audience: '…the Olympic Games are coming home tonight. This great, sport-loving country is widely recognised as the birthplace of modern sport.' Lord Coe, the Chair of the London Organising Committee for the Olympic Games and Paralympic Games (LOCOG), responded: 'Let us determine, all of us, all over the world, that London 2012 will see the best of us.'

Boyle kept his biggest surprise of all until last, when the Olympic Flame made its final journey from the Mayor of London's office to the Olympic Stadium. The biggest secret of all at an Olympic Games is who will light the Olympic Cauldron at the Opening Ceremony, and London 2012 was no exception. Speculation had been rife since London won the bid in 2005. As the moment of truth drew nearer, the money was still on Sir Steve Redgrave, winner of five gold medals in successive Games. Yet the bookies had reckoned without Boyle's ingenuity.

Held by footballer Jade Bailey, the Flame came up the River Thames on a high-powered speedboat, a magnificently windswept David Beckham at the helm. It was indeed Redgrave who carried the Flame from the boat into the Stadium, jogging through a guard of honour of 500 people who had worked on building the Olympic Park. So the beautiful, shining Olympic Torch, born aloft by Great Britain's brilliant Olympian rower, entered the arena for the last 400m of its 8,000-mile journey around the UK.

There was to be a final twist in the tail, however. No single person would light the Olympic Cauldron, but a group of seven young athletes, representing the generation to be inspired by the 2012 Olympic Games.

For the record – and we'll see how they perform in years to come – they were Callum Airlie (sailing), Jordan Duckitt (chairman of the London 2012 Young Ambassador Steering Group), Desiree Henry (athletics), Katie Kirk (athletics), Cameron MacRitchie (rowing), Aidan Reynolds (athletics) and Adelle Tracey (athletics). The seven youngsters took it in turns to carry the Flame as they jogged around the track until they reached their destination. There they found what the children in the athletes' parade had been carrying – 204 copper petals. From their Torches the young athletes each ignited a spark in one of the petals, allowing the Olympic Flame to spread gradually to the others. Then each in turn rose from the ground on long poles to form one great flower of a flame. The magnificent Olympic Cauldron, devised by the London-based designer Thomas Heatherwick, then took its place in the Olympic Stadium for the duration of the Games, only to be extinguished at the Closing Ceremony. After the Games the petals would return to each of the National Olympic Committees, a lasting reminder of their journey to London 2012.

No tricks, no archers, no acrobats, no thrills. This was dramatic and powerful, and the symbolism was clear. After a groundbreaking Opening Ceremony of so much fun and emotion, Boyle had brought the focus back to the flowering of youth, the inspiration of a generation at the heart of the original London bid. It was a great night's work by everyone involved, not least the thousands of volunteers who had practised routines for long hours and kept the secrets of the show so well. In its combination of thought-provoking action, humour and visual splendour, this 'different' Ceremony set the tone for the London 2012 Games to follow. And we all know how wonderful they turned out to be.

'To think that I stood on that podium where Ali and Frazier once stood and had their gold medals hung around their necks is just incredible.'

Nicola Adams, first women's Fly Weight Olympic gold medallist

5
FIRSTS OF LONDON 2012

Women Enter the Olympic Ring

The Sense of an Ending

Going for Gold

Women Enter the Olympic Ring

Gareth A Davies

*Women's Boxing joins the Olympic Games programme
after a long struggle for acceptance – and takes the
world by storm*

The stentorian crowd roared its approval: 'Ni-co-la,
Ni-co-la, Ni-co-la'. The wall of cacophonous sound was
for Britain's Nicola Adams, a will-o'-the-wisp figure, light
on her feet, dancing, as she challenged reigning world
champion Cancan Ren of China. It was round four of the
women's Olympic Fly Weight (51kg) final – and with less
than a minute remaining, Adams's dominance had set
her on course to become the first women's Boxing gold
medallist in Olympic history.

Adams, a 29-year-old from Leeds, had told me four
months before the Olympic Games that she believed once
millions of eyes witnessed women's Boxing in action there,
it would change forever the way in which the sport was
viewed. Now she had the chance to prove it. Only 5ft 5ins
tall, and weighing just under 51kgs, she extended her jab
with technical perfection and then unleashed a right cross
to follow. Then she did 'the Ali Shuffle', as a tilt to her
hero Muhammad Ali.

Boxing greats Sugar Ray Leonard and Muhammad Ali,
both of whom won Olympic gold medals, had fascinated

Adams from a young age. She'd even trained a few times in Sheffield at Naseem Hamed's old gym in Wincobank, and had enjoyed some sparring there. 'Leonard and Ali for me will always stay special,' she explained. 'Ali remains a brilliant man, and I do look to him for inspiration.' There were times when this was needed. A severe back injury in 2009 put Adams out of the game for a long time, and her return in June 2010 was to a tough tournament where she had to prove her worth.

The sweet science had captured Nicola's attention as a small child. Growing up on a diet of Frank Bruno bouts and videos of Leonard and Ali, she had taken up boxing aged 12. A year later she took part in her first amateur contest. At secondary school in Leeds she had been a formidable 100m and 200m sprinter, but once she had been to a gym, she revealed, 'that was it'. The only problem was that there was no one left to fight – no girls who wanted to step into the ring with her. For four years, between the ages of 13 and 17, it had been a case of 'sparring with lads' in the gym, and keeping her dreams alive. She could not find a female opponent with the will, or the skill, to stand with her.

Adams watched the rise and fall of Hamed, and then, aged 18, established herself as a leading British amateur. Those watching her at the Olympic Games marvelled as she disclosed the sacrifices she had made for the sport during the ten years leading up to London 2012. She admitted to never having held down a 'proper' job. She had stayed in further education until she was 24; she'd been a painter and decorator, and a tiler; she had fitted kitchens. Adams had even worked as an extra on the television soap operas *Coronation Street* and *Emmerdale*. All the while the gym had been her focus, and the idea of making a career from boxing was never far from her mind. That determination had paid off when in 2011, as European champion, Adams was placed on to the Lottery-funded programme.

The stage was set for Adams at London 2012. The inaugural women's Boxing competition included 36 women, 12 in each of the Fly Weight, Light Weight and Middle Weight divisions. Adams had a bye in the first round and then beat Bulgaria's Stoyka Petrova in the quarter-final. This brought her face to face with a legend, Chungneijang Mery Kom Hmangte of India, at the semi-final stage. Hmangte, five-time world champion since the women's world championships started in 2001, had come up two weight divisions to qualify for the competition.

Hmangte, who has become a role model for women across the sub-continent, is from Kangathei Village, a rural area of Churachandpur. She switched from athletics to boxing in 2000, discovering that she had been blessed with genetic gifts for boxing: fast hands, sublime balance and wonderful footwork. Her style in the ring, featuring wild left hands, is akin to that of an early Manny Pacquiao, and she has a great presence.

One of the darlings of the media, Hmangte also captured the headlines at London 2012, being several times overcome with emotion in interviews after her first bout. The 29-year-old sobbed her way joyfully through press conferences, explaining time and again the long, hard journey that women boxers had faced to take part in the Games. In the semi-final Adams proved herself too compact and too controlled for Hmangte, who returned to India with a bronze medal, and the knowledge that she had played a starring role in the first women's Olympic Boxing competition.

Adams had made it to the final. Waiting for her from the other half of the draw was Cancan Ren, who had beaten the Briton three months earlier, by a single point, in the world championship fly weight final. They were two boxers who many felt then would meet again, and so it proved.

With the Olympic final pitching Adams against her Chinese nemesis, spectators at ExCeL anticipated a memorable contest. They were not disappointed. The match was dominated by the Yorkshirewoman. Both competitors felt each other out early in the first round, then Adams landed a right and attacked. The world champion responded with an attack of her own. Then Adams, pop, pop, right, left. Light on her feet, looking for openings, it was an excellent first round display from the Briton. They tied up at the end of the round in a clinch, with Adams 4–2 up on the cards. In the second and third rounds Adams just got better, to lead first 9–4 and then 14–5. In the third round Adams showcased her skills while the proud Ren tried to come back, attempting to put Adams off her game plan with concerted attacks.

When the result was read out, 16–7 in her favour after four two-minute rounds, a smile burst across Adams's face that captured hearts and minds everywhere. It symbolised the exuberance of the entire women's Boxing competition at the Games. For Adams, who described her victory as a 'fairytale ending', it was a glorious finale. 'It is the pinnacle of my dreams, and I'm already thinking that I would love to go on and become double Olympic champion,' she laughed.

London 2012 saw admiration and awe in equal measure for the skills of a group of women who had finally found favour and were relishing their moment in the spotlight. Seventeen years of ambition, graft and sheer doggedness had earned Adams the right to smile. The final, which she described as 'the most compete performance'

▲ **1** The intricate frame of the Velodrome in its early stages of construction. The taut, economic structure features an incredibly light roof, around half that of any other covered velodrome.

▼ **2** An aerial view of the completed Olympic Park, the largest created for over a hundred years. Temporary and permanent venues blend with rivers, green lawns and wetlands, offering dramatic views over the city.

▲ **3** The World Shakespeare Festival included productions by many foreign theatre companies. Here the Habima Theatre company from Tel Aviv perform a Hebrew language version of *The Merchant of Venice* at London's Globe Theatre.

▼ **4** In the Iraqi Theatre Company's production of *Romeo and Juliet* in Baghdad, part of the World Shakespeare Festival, Romeo is Shiite and Juliet Sunni. Action unfolds against the haunting backdrop of not only feuding families, but a country torn by conflict and sectarian strife.

▲ **5** The Paralympic Torch Relay travelled through the night on a 92-mile journey from Stoke Mandeville to the Olympic Stadium. Here Torchbearer team members Greegan Clarkson, Caroline Baird and Argyle Bird carry the Paralympic Flame through Newham.

▼ **6** Craig Lundberg, who lost his sight serving in Iraq in 2007, is delighted to represent the city of Liverpool as he takes a ferry across the Mersey en route to the Evening Celebration on the Pier Head. 'I only hope I've done them proud,' he said.

▲ **7** A magnificent peal from Britain's newly cast Olympic Bell, the largest in Europe at 27 tonnes, marks the start of the Olympic Opening Ceremony. The Bell, engraved with the words 'Be not afeard, the isle is full of noises' from Shakespeare's *The Tempest*, was struck at 9pm on 27 July by Team GB cyclist Bradley Wiggins.

▲ **8** Flagbearer Peter Norfolk, a Wheelchair Tennis legend, becomes the first athlete ever to lead ParalympicsGB into the Opening Ceremony of a home Paralympic Games. He described the experience of entering the Olympic Stadium as 'utterly wonderful … utterly amazing'.

▼ **9** The Olympic Cauldron, designed by Thomas Heatherwick, brings the Opening Ceremony to a spectacular conclusion. Its 204 copper petals, one for each competing nation, rose from the ground on poles to create a beautiful flaming flower.

▲ **10** Team GB's Nicola Adams celebrates winning the first-ever Olympic women's Boxing final over China's Cancan Ren. She described taking the Fly Weight (51kg) gold medal as a 'fairytale ending' to her remarkable campaign.

▼ **11** Katherine Grainger (right) kisses her gold medal as she and Anna Watkins celebrate their emphatic win in the women's Double Sculls final at Eton Dorney. It was the second gold medal for the Great British Rowing team at London 2012, in a regatta that eventually led to nine medals for the team, four of them gold.

▲ **12** Michael Phelps powers to the final gold medal of an outstanding career as he brings the USA team home in the 4 x 100m Medley Relay. Retiring as the most decorated Olympian of all time, the swimmer also holds the record for gold medals overall and gold medals awarded for individual events.

▲ **13** Peter Charles and his horse Vindicat secure victory for Great Britain in a dramatic jump-off against the Netherlands to decide the Team Jumping gold medal. Vindicat overcame an inconsistent start to the competition to jump a clear round when it mattered most.

of her career, had happened as she had dreamt it, and afterwards she beat her heart with her gloved fist in joy.

Over the following days the public peered in at a new sporting hero, with a million-dollar smile. They learned about Dexter, her pet Doberman, who had watched her on screen from the kennels during the event. More sobering were the details of a back injury in 2011, sustained when she tripped over her handwraps and fell down the stairs at home. Forced into bed for three months, she was unable to move, leaving the Team GB doctor, Mike Loosemore, seriously concerned. 'Nicola went from 300 sit-ups a day to being unable to lift her shoulders off the bed,' he explained. 'Never mind getting to the Olympic Games, there was a point when I thought she might never walk again.' The depth of her determination was a fitting tribute to a sport that had battled so hard to enter Olympic competition.

Sunday 5 August, Day Nine of the Games, saw the start of the inaugural women's Olympic Boxing competition. Just after 1.30pm, the first women boxers entered the ring for the first time in Olympic history. It had taken 116 years, but at last two Fly Weights, Elena Savelyeva of the Russian Federation and Hye Song Kim of the Democratic People's Republic of Korea, could begin their skilful combat. A veil was lifted, a stigma removed, as the women engaged toe-to-toe, dancing back and forth, for the four two-minute rounds. From the press tribunes, in their vests and headguards, it might have been two men in the ring. There was little difference in skill, movement, agility or intent. The audience saw it immediately, and the public, largely, took to the sport overnight.

Without question the arrival of women's Boxing heralded a seminal moment in sport, and a huge achievement for the competitors. Over four days 36 women punched a gaping hole in prejudice and preconception. Many of them had vast experience, others were relatively new to the sport, but all relished the chance to take part and shape its future. Several became overnight stars under a more intense media spotlight than anything they had known before. Nicola Adams, Ireland's Katie Taylor at Light Weight and 17-year-old Claressa Shields of the USA in Middle Weight were the iconic champions in the three weight divisions.

One woman in the audience took special pleasure in seeing women's Boxing flourish under the oxygen of Olympic publicity. 'Eyes on the sport was always going to be the key,' noted pioneer Barbara Buttrick, ringside at ExCeL for the opening on Day Nine. Known as 'The Mighty Atom' and standing at 4ft 11ins, she had been pilloried in national newspapers when she began to box in the late 1940s. The reception at the London 2012 Games could not have afforded greater contrast, to Buttrick's delight. 'This will set the sport off for women around the world,' she reflected proudly.

Buttrick boxed in fairground booths, having taken part for the first time in 1949 on the Epsom Downs on Derby Day. In 1952 she went to the United States, where promoters were prepared to include women in the shows. 'I wanted to be here for the first-ever day of women's Boxing at the Olympic Games,' said the 82-year-old, who described the development as a 'landmark moment' that would transform perception of her sport. 'The Olympic Games will give women boxers credibility and the public will begin to accept them,' she predicted – and what transpired over the four sessions turned her comments into an understatement.

The impact of women's Boxing was greater than anyone could have imagined. The venue at ExCeL was sold out, day after day. There was razzamatazz and music, ring walks to iconic soundtracks, and every session was an event in itself. On Day 10 of the Games Ireland's four-time world champion Katie Taylor took on GB's Natasha Jonas, the first British woman ever to win an Olympic Boxing match, in the Light Weight quarter-final. The noise level at their event was recorded at 113.7 decibels, the loudest of any venue anywhere at the Games. One professional promoter wagered that he could put the 25-year-old Taylor on in a stadium in Ireland and could fill it with 60,000 to 80,000 spectators.

Where boxing was traditionally, for many men, an escape from poverty, the pattern is being repeated for women in developing countries. In China, twenty-four regional squads are in training to create an elite. In India the diminutive Hmangte, who weighs just 7st 3lbs, has earned herself a physical instructor's role in the police department and a government-built bungalow. Her husband, a former professional footballer, supports her sports career, although her parents had been less enthusiastic. When Hmangte won the state championship in her early twenties, a photograph appeared in a local newspaper. Hmangte, who had not told her parents that she was boxing, was castigated by her father, who insisted it was taboo for women to compete in the sport. Reaching the Olympic Games, however, remained her ultimate dream.

Hmangte's experience is being mirrored across the developing world, where boxing can be an empowering sport for those who succeed. In India, groups of women from rural areas are attending boxing camps run by the Government. If they become a national team athlete, they may also secure government jobs, military posts, positions in the police fore or with India's vast rail network.

Bringing women's Boxing into the Games has been one of the major legacies of Dr Ching-Kuo Wu, president of the Amateur International Boxing Association. 'After many years of development, the women have shown that they have the standard, the skills, fighting spirit and sportsmanship to be included in the Olympic movement,' he told me. Wu anticipates a 'very bright' future for the sport, noting that of the 196 National Federations overall, 120 now feature women's programmes, and more are expected to follow. 'London was a good place to start and prove the popularity of women's Boxing,' he commented, adding that he hoped to include more divisions at Rio 2016 and beyond. The 36 trailblazing female boxers of London 2012 are only the beginning, with more opportunities opening up for competitors all the time.

Olympic champion Nicola Adams is already contemplating Rio 2016. The amateur set-up is strong and, after Great Britain finished the Games at the top of the Boxing medals table (with three gold, one silver and one bronze medal), funding will be enhanced for the class of 2016. 'Rio 2016 is definitely an option for me. We've never had a double female Olympic champion in Boxing, and there is definitely a motivation there,' she said.

The professional ranks are also an option, but are currently less likely. One reason is that Adams is a technical, clinical boxer, a style more suited to the amateur ranks. Another is that women's professional boxing remains, at best, piecemeal and embryonic. Adams has other goals, too. She is seeking to be a beacon for those wishing to change their lives by taking up the sport. 'I'm hoping that the Olympic Games in London has inspired more youngsters to get in at grass-roots level and come up through the ranks and be where we are now.'

So the Olympic Games are over for another four years, by which time the burgeoning sport will surely have come a long way. For Adams, London 2012 brought her a fairy-tale ending that she had dreamed of since the age of 12. 'To think that I stood on that podium where Ali and Frazier once stood and had their gold medals hung around their necks is just incredible,' she observes. For many other women, already boxing or newly entering the sport, she and the other medallists will provide an inspiration, proof that talent and dedication can deliver magnificent results. And for many new fans of women's Boxing, an abiding memory of the Olympic Games will be of seeing Adams perform. Quick-thinking and light on her feet, she took the fight to Cancan Ren, the counter-puncher from China who had defeated her in the world championship final only three months earlier. Adams, the new 'Mighty Atom', combining skilful moves in the ring with brilliant smiles for the crowd, emphasised to thousands of spectators across the world why women deserve the right to box.

The Sense of an Ending

Kate Battersby

Peter Norfolk, ParalympicsGB's Flagbearer in the Paralympic Games Opening Ceremony, takes a surprise silver in the Quad Doubles

Some moments in life are incomparable. Peter Norfolk has had more than his share. At 19, a motorcycle crash put him in Britain's world-renowned Stoke Mandeville Hospital for more than a year and left him a paraplegic. At 30, he discovered wheelchair tennis in a big way. At 39, a further deterioration in his condition caused him to lose function in his right arm, requiring him to have a tennis racket strapped to his hand in order to play the sport, now in the Quad classification. He was 43 when Wheelchair Tennis was introduced to the Athens 2004 Paralympic Games, where he took the inaugural gold in the Quad Singles and silver in the Quad Doubles with Mark Eccleston. One week after that incredible high, he and his wife Louise lost their first baby. Norfolk is a man who knows about perspective.

Yet the landmarks kept coming. At Beijing 2008 he retained his Quad Singles gold and took Quad Doubles bronze with Jamie Burdekin – and later that year he and Louise welcomed their son Joseph into the world. Daughter Evie followed in 2010, even as Norfolk amassed wheelchair tennis crown after wheelchair tennis crown. By the summer of London 2012, he had won five Australian Opens, two US Opens, 13 Super Series tournaments, finishing the year as world number one on five occasions. At the age of 51, he was a quad tennis legend. He even bore a nickname befitting such status: 'the Quadfather'.

By the time he was, of course, selected for the Quad Singles and Doubles as part of the ten-strong British Wheelchair Tennis team at London 2012, Norfolk's was already a career of many landmarks and highlights. Yet nothing in his professional life would ever compare to the moment at 10.48pm on the night of Wednesday 29 August – the instant when he led the ParalympicsGB team into the Olympic Stadium, with the unmatched honour of being his nation's Flagbearer, elected by his fellow 300 teammates.

Few athletes win Paralympic gold. Fewer still have the chance to carry their country's flag in a Paralympic Games Opening Ceremony. Barely any do this on their own national turf. Never, before the night of 29 August 2012, had a British Paralympian carried the Union flag into Britain's Olympic Stadium at the head of the British Paralympic team. Now just one person on the planet could make that claim. One man. One moment in history. That moment belonged to Peter Norfolk.

The Olympic Stadium was packed with 80,000 people, almost all of whom had been waiting for this exceptional point in the Opening Ceremony. Already 163 competing nations had been introduced, with representatives of the 4,294 athletes taking part welcomed warmly by the huge crowd. Already it was known that this would be a Paralympic Games like none before it – the largest and most commercially successful in history. But in this Opening Ceremony it was manifest that for the first time the Paralympic Games had true, acknowledged parity with its sister event. When ParalympicsGB was introduced the wall of sound produced by 80,000 voices had to be heard to be believed.

Norfolk himself had trouble taking it in, so overwhelmed were his senses. He moved his chair forward, the Union flag planted firmly next to him, the wheels of his chair – like all those of his similarly powered teammates – also emblazoned with the national emblem. The stadium exploded with sound and colour. The David Bowie track *Heroes*, the signature song of all Britain's competitors at London 2012, burst from the public address system. No Paralympian had ever heard anything like this before.

Norfolk gazed around as he led the team along the track. He saw the applause of HM The Queen and other members of the Royal Family, the standing ovation of the Prime Minister and members of the Government, of international heads of State, of 80,000 lovers of elite sport who cheered and waved in salute. 'It was utterly fantastic,' Norfolk told the record British television audience later, speaking live on air after the lighting of the Paralympic Cauldron. 'I've never done anything like that. I've never experienced anything so utterly wonderful – the fireworks, the Queen here, all the athletes... What a start to our Games. It's going to be sensational.'

Later still, on his Twitter feed, Norfolk added, 'That was totally fantastic! What a welcome. Thanks everyone for your support. Utterly amazing. What a reception from the Stadium crowd for ParalympicsGB. I am so proud to lead out all our exceptional athletes. Good luck, everyone!'

It was unusual to hear Norfolk speak with such mellow emotion, known as he is for not suffering fools gladly. Occasionally he is not one to suffer anyone gladly. 'I'm very argumentative. Abrasive. Arrogant. And I don't like losing. I just want to win every match I play,' he admits. You don't get to be the best quad player on the planet any other way – quad, incidentally, meaning reduced feeling and/or function in three or more limbs as a result of a higher spinal cord injury than that of a paraplegic. Norfolk himself likes clarity on the subject. 'I'm a T4/C8 incomplete, not a quadriplegic,' he explains in interviews. 'Terminology is very important. The biggest mistake people make is to think I'm disabled from the waist down. The C8 bit affects the nerves of my right arm. I can't grip the racket unaided and I need it strapped to my hand. I'm also T4, meaning I don't have any trunk stability either.'

In regular life Norfolk also runs his own business, selling specialist equipment for the physically challenged.

'It's great that wheelchair tennis is about your ability, not your disability,' he emphasises. 'Paralympians should be defined as athletes, not disabled. I just happen to be in a chair.' Norfolk is, as is obvious, what journalists call 'a good quote'. They like interviewing him because he says interesting things, frequently peppered with the same colourful language that scorches the court during his training sessions. Nothing if not an engaging talker, he has never been interested in being a vacuous 'personality'. Norfolk wants respect, quite simply because he feels his sport merits it. 'It helps that the professional Tour players respect what we do,' he says. 'We don't receive or expect the same money although we put in the same commitment. But I compete for my own pride. I want to stay number one. I want gold again.'

At the Paralympic Games there were two clear days between the Opening Ceremony and the start of the Wheelchair Tennis programme. In the meantime Norfolk was clearly enthralled by the Paralympic experience on home soil, enthusiastically tweeting support for his gold medal winning teammates David Weir and Hannah Cockcroft in their Athletics track events. 'What a fabulous atmosphere, wandering around the Olympic Park meeting all the Paralympic Games sports fans,' he added. 'Keep on cheering Team GB.'

The Wheelchair Tennis took place at Eton Manor at the northernmost point of the Olympic Park – uniquely the only venue constructed especially for the Paralympic Games. Norfolk welcomed the fact that, in contrast to the Olympic competition, the Wheelchair Tennis was not in faraway south west London on Wimbledon's hallowed lawns. He preferred being inside the Olympic Park itself, relishing its intimacy and atmosphere. Besides, the Eton Manor facility was seriously impressive. The 27-acre site contained nine competition courts and four practice courts, boasting 10,500 spectator seats including a 5,000-capacity centre court. Norfolk knew this would be his toughest tournament ever, such was the increasing depth in the Quad game. He had not had a flawless year, but his mind was set on the Paralympic Games. 'I've had a bad few months, but I'm not going to have a bad Eton Manor,' he pledged. 'I get butterflies just talking about winning gold in London. I can't tell you much I really want to do it.'

Both his Quad Singles and Doubles campaigns began well. Seeded three, he got the Quad Singles underway with a 6–0 6–0 'double bagel' whitewash over the world number 19, Mitsuteru Moroishi. The Japanese would also fall to Norfolk in the Quad Doubles, as he and partner Shota Kawano were defeated by Norfolk and Andy Lapthorne, the number one seeds, 6–2 6–2 in the semifinals after the Britons had a first-round bye.

'We'll win the final I'm sure, whoever we play,' Norfolk forecast confidently. 'The whole Games have been absolutely amazing so far and I'm so proud to be a part of it and to have secured a medal. I was really nervous, but I'm so happy to win and at least go one better than at Beijing 2008. Andy was definitely the dominant player and he kept us in there and hit some great shots.'

But then came the shock of the competition. On Wednesday 4 September Norfolk was first up on Court One, with his Quad Singles quarter-final against Israel's Shraga Weinberg beginning at 11am. It did not suit the Briton. The first set went his way, but in the second he served 12 double faults and never regained control of the match. Weinberg, world number one in 2001 but now ranked just ten, won 3–6 7–5 6–0. Norfolk was not sanguine in defeat. 'Appalling,' he said afterwards. 'Shraga played okay. But my grip went and I couldn't hit the ball back in the court. If you don't do that, you can't win. There wasn't a lot I could do. It was a combination of tape and loss of strength when I went to swing. But it's no excuse.'

The great Paralympian was left with only the Quad Doubles final to look forward to, in which he and Lapthorne were to face David Wagner and Nick Taylor, defending champions from the USA. 'I should be ready for that,' insisted Norfolk. 'I'm looking forward to it … it's almost a con-solation. I'm disappointed I didn't get into a medal position to defend my Singles title. I came up short.'

So the Quad Doubles still beckoned – perhaps this was to be Norfolk's destiny. He had already won Paralympic bronze and silver in the event. Maybe this was where he was fated to win a gold medal in 2012. But elite sport is rarely so obliging with medal symmetry. Fairytales, despite the headlines, are relatively rare. Sometimes it's just not your time; sometimes it's just someone else's story.

Norfolk and Lapthorne lost. They fought back from a set and 3–1 down to force a decider, and for a while it seemed that an epic victory might be possible. But from 2–2 in the third set, the match rapidly went away from them. The Americans won 6–2 5–7 6–2 to retain their Paralympic crown. 'We didn't really deliver and from a tennis perspective we could have done more, but it is all about on the day and we didn't do it,' Norfolk reflected. 'The Americans played a very solid game and you can't take that away from them. We thought the third set was ours for the taking, but sometimes you can't turn it around.'

Lapthorne, at 21 making his Paralympic Games debut, was bitterly disappointed with the defeat, the pair's silver medal providing little consolation. 'Hopefully I will have more Games after this, but I tried so hard for Peter and I am absolutely gutted,' he said. 'We are the best team in the world but it just wasn't meant to be today.'

There was a charming scene on court after the final, when Norfolk's two young children ran to hug him, to be greeted with a smile and outstretched arms. With a family, he is increasingly aware that competition cannot remain his priority for his entire life. Nothing is decided. 'I still think I am the best player in the world and we will see whether I continue to the next Paralympic Games at Rio 2016,' he said. 'I haven't stopped playing for 12 years and I will definitely be taking a break. I have a young family and I want to spend time with them.'

So London 2012 was not, after all, to be a golden Games for Norfolk. After 20 years of elite wheelchair tennis, the Quadfather's dominance had been eclipsed. Yet he had had his epiphany. Nothing could ever obliterate the extraordinary reception that he had experienced at the Opening Ceremony as his nation's Flagbearer. And his moving final thoughts on London 2012 were not of disappointment, but rather of unbridled pride. 'A big "thank you" to everyone for your love and support,' he tweeted. 'I am so proud to be a part of the greatest team, full of awe-inspiring athletes.'

And none of it could ever have been possible had his life not been altered beyond imagining in 1979, when he was 19, with the motorbike smash which led to his wheelchair tennis career. 'If I could change it now I probably wouldn't,' Norfolk said of his paraplegia. 'I would never have achieved so much, travelled as much or had my own business. I have a very full life which I'm extremely grateful for. But it took me quite a few years to reach that point … Yes, I could have another deterioration and lose the function in my left hand too. But I don't fear it. I live for the day. What will be will be. I'm happy I've overcome whatever it is.'

ParalympicsGB could have had no better Flagbearer. Norfolk has travelled a long road to London 2012 – embracing life and death, achievement and loss. His drive and determination are remarkable. They have carried him to an incredible level of success and respect among his fellow athletes who know, none better, the knife edge upon which success and defeat, participation and retirement can reside. Only a few win Paralympic gold. Fewer still carry their national flag at an Opening Ceremony. Just one man on the planet has borne the Union flag into a UK Olympic Stadium at the start of a Paralympic Games … Peter Norfolk. The Quadfather. A dominant figure in wheelchair tennis, he has undoubtedly inspired a generation, as London 2012 desired.

Going for Gold

Craig Lord

*Michael Phelps swims to Olympic history in his
swansong Games*

Had time finally caught up with the master of timing?
Had the Midas touch abandoned the most golden of all
Olympians? Even those who had followed the amazing trajectory of Michael Phelps, from 15-year-old finalist
at Sydney 2000 to winner of a record eight gold medals
at Beijing 2008, started to wonder as they watched the
American miss the Victory podium for the first time in any
race at three Olympic Games.

It was Day One at the London 2012 Aquatics Centre, in
the midst of a session delivering upset at every turn. Now
the 27-year-old legend, with six golds from Athens 2004
and eight from Beijing 2008 in tow, finished fourth in the
400m Individual Medley.

Perhaps heir apparent and teammate Ryan Lochte, his
first gold medal of the Games in the bag, had been right
all along when he predicted 'this is my time'. It certainly
seemed that way as Phelps spoke of his struggle with
'heavy legs' that left him four seconds shy of his teammate and the wrong side of Brazil's Thiago Pereira and
Japan's Kosuke Hagino.

Phelps' time from US trials a month earlier would have won him silver by a second. But in both performance and demeanour after the London race, the most decorated swimmer in history looked far more ready to join the ranks of greats who had tried and failed than the triple-crown club of those who came, conquered and came back to conquer again and again.

Just two swimmers, both women, had ever won the same race in the pool at three Olympic Games. Australian Dawn Fraser did so over 100m Freestyle at Tokyo 1964, becoming the founder member of that illustrious group. In 1996 she was joined by Hungarian Krisztina Egerszegi over 200m Backstroke. At London 2012 Phelps and Japan's Kosuke Kitajima had six chances of membership between them. The race was on.

The second day brought a ray of hope for Phelps. Kitajima's miss in the 100m Breaststroke left the door ajar for Phelps to be the first man to win the triple. Although the USA had to settle for silver behind France in a nail-biting 4 x 100m Freestyle Relay, its biggest hitter looked sharp ahead of the one race few thought he could lose: his signature 200m Butterfly.

This was the event in which Michael Phelps had made the Olympic Games at 15, in which he had made the Olympic final and finished fifth at Sydney 2000. He set his first world record in this event, again aged 15, in spring 2001. He would break the mark seven times in all and between 2003 and 2012 he never lost an important race over 200m Butterfly. 'It's home for me,' Phelps once said of the four-length 'fly race that had brought him gold at the 2004 and 2008 Olympic Games.

All of which counted for little as he lined up for the final at London 2012. His rivals' keenest memory was the sight of Phelps being beaten three days earlier over the 400m Individual Medley. They smelled blood. That much was obvious as Chad Le Clos of South Africa and Takeshi Matsuda of Japan stuck to the champion like glue down the first three legs of the final.

Phelps looked strong, but a poor last turn proved a mistake he could not afford to make. Le Clos, a 20-year-old who sensed that the king could be toppled, clawed into contention with each passing stroke. With two metres to go he lunged for the kill, taking the crown by 0.05 in 1:52.96. Phelps, 0.2 ahead of Matsuda who took bronze, looked dejected. He was courteous to Le Clos, but the flash of anger and frustration on his face were critical clues to what was to follow.

Less than an hour after this defeat there was some consolation for Phelps. Gold in the 4 x 200m Freestyle Relay delivered a 19th career medal that took him one honour beyond the all-time record of 18 that had been held by the Russian gymnast Larisa Latynina since 1964. It also turned the tide on his own grand finale.

Phelps was subsequently buoyed by meeting Latynina and receiving a medal that had been given to her by the USA at a Russia v America gymnastics duel at the height of the Cold War. The day after missing his second chance to become the first man in the triple crown club, the swimming phenomenon drew on two of his great assets: his ability to take a hard knock and convert it to fuel for the next fight, and his ability to conserve energy wherever he can in the midst of a demanding multi-event programme.

Ryan Lochte lost his 200m Backstroke crown by a touch to fellow-American Tyler Clary and Japan's Ryosuke Irie. Even as his campaign began to wane, Phelps' began to gather momentum, and on 2 August his Midas touch returned on a full moon. Defeated by Lochte in the 200m medley at the world championships in 2011, Phelps exploited his teammate's weakness. The defending champion controlled the 200m Individual Medley from gun to gold, with Lochte unable to cope with the punishing opening pace that Phelps set. He duly stamped his triple-crown card in 1:54.27, finishing 0.63 ahead of Lochte. He had done it. Phelps had taken his first solo gold medal of his swansong Games.

It was truly 'game back on'. Half an hour later Phelps issued a 50.86 warning that booked lane four for the final of the 100m Butterfly. This was another race in which he could enter yet another line in a history book already groaning with Phelpsian entries. No swimmer had ever won three crowns in more than one event.

By the close of the penultimate day of Phelps' racing career, one man had. An unrelenting 51.21 effort in the 100m Butterfly final delivered Phelps his 17th Olympic career gold and his 21st medal of any colour. At London 2012 a fourth place and two silvers had been well and truly outshone by three straight golds. The swansong was now in tune with the ambition of Phelps' coach Bob Bowman. All season he had been humming Dvořák's 7th Symphony, believing that it reflected Phelps' final mission as a swimmer. Composed in 1884 with a London premiere in mind, the work is redolent, said the coach, of 'sentimentality, melancholy, sadness, struggle, defiant triumph and legacy'.

The last masterstroke of Phelps' career unfolded on the last day of action in the Aquatics Centre pool, as the keeper of American tradition in the 4 x 100m Medley Relay. The USA had won every title for which it had raced since 1960 – a record stretching back over 50 years.

Phelps, together with Matt Grevers, Brendan Hansen and Nathan Adrian, did not let the side down.

It was a tally to end them all: 22 Olympic medals, 18 of them gold. This was more than twice the number of ultimate prizes awarded to the next-most-decorated winners of all time: runner Paavo Nurmi of Finland, gymnast Larisa Latynina of the USSR, swimmer Mark Spitz of the USA and sprinter Carl Lewis, also of the USA, from Athletics.

How did the champion feel as he walked away from the sport that had dominated his life? Phelps was unsurprisingly tearful as he stepped on to the Olympic podium one last time, on his way to the tallest plinth in the pantheon of Olympic greats. The emotion of the evening was intense. 'It's tough to put into words right now. I did everything I wanted to and finished how I wanted to,' said Phelps.

The magnificent athlete showed perspective, too, aware that this had been a journey for several people. When Phelps finished his last warm-up, he looked up from the water, peered through his goggles at coach Bob Bowman and said, 'I have looked up to Michael Jordan all my life. He became the best basketball player there ever was. I've been able to become the best swimmer of all time; we got here together. Thank you.'

If Phelps restricted his status to 'best swimmer', others did not. The International Swimming Federation presented him with a trophy engraved with the words: 'To Michael Phelps, The greatest Olympic athlete of all time, From FINA'. The debate over his candidacy as 'the greatest Olympian' may well continue, but his versatility and power in the pool went well beyond anything the sport had ever seen before. Michael Phelps' remarkable accomplishments included 37 world records (he retired as standard bearer in six events, including the 100m and 200m Butterfly, the 400m Medley and all three Relays).

The story of a boy who sported a 2.01m arm span to outstretch his 1.96m height broke the mould. When one first reflects upon America and swimming, the mind wanders from Baywatch and beach babes to California beaches and the birthplace of Mark Spitz – he of the moustache, the golden smile and tan to match, hero of a sport for the landed and loaded with ocean views and time and talent to spare.

Think again. Try a working-class world away: Baltimore, Babe Ruth, broken home, burning ambition, back-breaking regime, a boy with a breathtaking talent. Think big. Think Michael Fred Phelps. Not seven laurels, but eight. No limits. 'You can't put a limit on anything,' said Phelps at 23, heading into his third Olympic campaign. 'The more you dream, the farther you get.'

Phelps was born in the blue-collar mill town of Towson on the north-east coast of Maryland, where dreams are made on football fields and not in water. The third and youngest child of Fred, a state trooper, and Debbie, a school administrator and teacher, he followed sisters Hilary and Whitney to the North Baltimore Aquatics club, headed by coach Bowman.

Separated and reconciled before Michael was born, Fred and Debbie made the final split just as their seven-year-old son started to swim competitively, and it was Phelps' mother who steered the often challenging champion-to-be. 'In kindergarten I was told by his teacher, "Michael can't sit still, Michael can't be quiet, Michael can't focus",' she later recalled. 'I said, maybe he's bored. The teacher replied, "He's not gifted. Your son will never be able to focus on anything."' Some mistakes stand out more than others.

Phelps was diagnosed with ADHD – attention deficit hyperactivity disorder. He was put on permanent medication, but after two years he refused to take it. On his own and in the pool, he focused his energy. When Phelps was 11 Bowman took Debbie aside and gave her his predictions. 'By 2000, I look for him to be in the Olympic trials. By 2004, he makes the Olympics. By 2008, he'll set world records. By 2012, the Olympics will be in New York and…' Bowman had spotted something rare in his pool, a boy who said 'I don't get tired', even though he was swimming beyond his years.

'I think that probably the thing that maybe I'm most proud of is that he has such a thorough understanding of the process of success. He knows how to set a goal, figure out the steps it will take to get there, come up with a plan and stick to it whether things are easy or hard,' said the coach. 'Michael's mind is like a clock. He can go into the 200m butterfly knowing he needs to do the first 50 in 24.6 to break the record, and can put that time in his head and make his body do 24.6 exactly,' his mother revealed. Even as a child Phelps always did his swimming homework, watching tapes from his international races with his mother over dinner.

For Bowman, such dedication was an immense strength in one so young. 'One of the things I call Michael is the motivation machine,' he explained. 'Bad moods, good moods, he channels everything for gain. He's motivated by success, he loves to swim fast and when he does that he goes back and trains better. He's motivated by failure, by money, by people saying things about him … just anything that comes along he turns into a reason to train harder, swim better. Channelling his energy is one of his greatest attributes.'

Bowman discovered hidden depths to Phelps early on. 'He's had the same mental approach since he was very young ... he's able to block everything out.' Asked what made Phelps so good, his response was simple. 'His mind ... his ability to focus under the maximum pressure and get the most out of his body. He gets the maximum performance when the stakes are at the highest.'

The coach could be severe as he pushed his protégé forward. He trod on the 12-year-old's goggles to teach him that he could race without them; he asked the bus driver to come to the pool late after competition so that the hotel kitchen would have closed by the time Phelps got back to eat. He got the boy to race not only his own races, but also the relays in every age group at youth meets, seven or eight races in a session until Michael could take no more. 'I just think that I wanted him to be prepared for any situation that came up,' says Bowman. 'It was expecting the best possible result when he's in the worst possible situation.'

Bowman now has some 2,000 children going through North Baltimore Aquatic's swimming lessons each season. Could there be another Michael out there? He resists the idea, reluctant to 'curse people with that expectation'. For Phelps' immense physical talent combined with unique mental focus to create a truly extraordinary athlete. Born to push boundaries, he became the first swimmer in Olympic history to win three golds in more than one Games, and for many will always be 'the greatest Olympic athlete of all time'. At London 2012, his most challenging and yet most triumphant Games, he created moments of astonishing drama. It was a privilege to have seen Michael Phelps in action, a sporting genius making his own legend.

'There was a job to do. I and my great teammates had spent seven years preparing to win an Olympic gold medal. Provided I didn't disrupt the team, I had to rejoin them.'

Kate Walsh, captain of Team GB women's Hockey team

6

GREAT TEAM EFFORTS

On Golden Pond

Andrew Longmore

Eton Dorney hosts the best regatta ever for GB's Olympic Rowing team

If only his legs would stop shaking, Andrew Triggs Hodge thought he might be able to win another Olympic gold medal for Britain. But they wouldn't. For five minutes after pushing off from the pontoon for the biggest race of his life Triggs Hodge, the stroke of the GB Four, was quivering like a big jelly. This hadn't happened at Beijing 2008 when they had won the Olympic title, nor in school or at university, nor even before he had led the Dark Blues to victory in the Oxford and Cambridge Boat Race. Behind him Tom James, Pete Reed and Alex Gregory were also trying to cope with a nauseous brew of fear and anticipation. Gregory, the only member of the crew without a gold medal to his name, had already thrown up, perpetuating a tradition established over a number of Olympic finals by Matthew Pinsent.

It took a few practice starts and a number of minutes before Triggs Hodge regained control of his lower body and began to coax himself into a feeling of sublime invincibility, the mood in which he liked to race. He remembered the excitement from Beijing 2008, relishing the sense of looming pain and battle. He had known he was on the right side four years ago and, though the Australians were a powerful and classy crew, he was sure he was this time as well. For a start, 25,000 people were lining the Eton Dorney course, the biggest crowd ever experienced in a sport such as Rowing, and many would be rooting for Team GB. All week, a succession of gold medal winners had spoken in awe of the wall of sound that had washed over them at the 400m mark, a tidal wave of hope to lift them across the line. The level of home support was unprecedented, but the pressure was on. Deprived of their Olympic title in the last few metres of the Lightweight Double Sculls, Mark Hunter and Zac Purchase had barely managed to mumble an apology to the crowd before collapsing in despair. 'We feel we've let everyone down,' Hunter said. The rest of the interview was submerged by tears, from the rowers and from the interviewer. Rowing, mostly a distant, detached, sport, reveals a very different face to spectators during the Olympic Games.

Usually the beat of an Olympic regatta starts steadily and quickens through the week until a deafening clash of cymbals heralds the finals over the last two days. At London 2012, however, the finals were spread out across four days, with the Eights moved from their usual slot as the last race on the last day to the first day of the finals on Wednesday. Two unexpected benefits emerged from the new-look schedule. One was that Britain's assertion of dominance over their home lake, which had begun with a historic first gold for Heather Stanning and Helen Glover in the women's Pair and continued with an impossibly emotional victory for Katherine Grainger and Anna Watkins two days later in the women's Double Sculls, became a ritual drawn out over several days. Rival teams had to endure a lot of British cheering. The second was that the GB Eight became the barometer for the performance of the whole team – both statistically, because each of the men's crews match themselves against one another in training every day, and psychologically, because they could lay down a marker for the rest of the British team and for all the other nations. How would the British boat cope under the pressure and expectation of a home Olympic Games?

After a frustrating four years spent mostly in the wash of the world champion German crew, the GB Eight had come to the point of no return. They had yet to beat the Germans; no one, in fact, had beaten the Germans since the Beijing 2008 Games. Occasionally the GB Eight had come close; mostly, they had been a distant second. But they were probably the second-best crew in the six-boat final, which meant that they could plan their race logically around the aim of winning silver. No disgrace there. Except that they planned nothing of the sort. Like the victorious – and now legendary – GB Eight at Sydney 2000, there was no prize other than gold. Go out there, try to break the Germans and win the race. In doing so, they risked losing everything.

Greg Searle had returned to Rowing to win gold at the age of 40, 20 years after he and his brother Jonny had won the Coxed Pairs at Barcelona 1992. Searle could also have told everyone about the heartache of coming fourth. With Ed Coode, he had led the Pairs race to 1500m at Sydney 2000, only to be rowed out of the medals in the final strokes. It was partly that feeling of despair, of unfinished business, that had lured him back to a life in which unfurling his back became a major ritual in the morning and reaching down to put on his socks an Olympic achievement. But Searle had not suspended his working and family life just to win a silver. He had come back to win gold. Searle's voice would have been influential in the decision to go for broke, but Ric Egington, a no-nonsense northerner, and Mo Sbihi, the first Muslim to row for Britain, as well as the prodigiously talented young stroke Constantine Louloudis were all equally clear about the strategy. The GB Eight would race its heart out to 1500m and then hang on for dear life. And it so nearly worked. Neck and neck with the Germans for three-quarters of the 2km course, the home challenge only faltered inside the last 400m. Tiring now with every stroke, the GB Eight was cut down by the Canadians who slipped past for silver medal; they would have lost bronze as well had not the finishing line arrived just in time. The Canadians, the deposed Olympic champions, celebrated as if they had won back their title; across the way from the Media Centre, in an area reserved for athletes and their families that became known as the 'kiss and cry zone', Stan Louloudis fingered the bronze medal hanging round his neck and didn't know what to think. Olympic bronze was not bad for a 21-year-old, but how much better could it have been?

Back at the British team's headquarters at Oakley Court on a quiet tributary of the Thames, the heroics of the GB Eight had certainly not gone unnoticed, least of all by Triggs Hodge and his Four. 'The way they attacked that race was hugely inspirational,' he said later. 'They knew the risks involved and they sacrificed a silver to win gold. How do you do that? By putting yourself in a position to win gold. Unfortunately it cost them.' Thankfully, only a silver.

Every day back at the hotel the medallists were filing in, some with gold, some silver, a few bronze. On the Wednesday Heather Stanning, a captain in the Royal Artillery on secondment to GB Rowing, and Helen Glover, a confident, outgoing product of the Sporting Giants programme (she had to stand on tiptoe to reach the five feet 10inch qualification height), had claimed the team's first gold. Glover had only begun rowing four years ago after watching the Beijing 2008 Olympic Games on television, yet the pair had dominated the season, winning all three world cups and transferring their form to the Olympic Games with an infectious confidence. Watching the Pair storm off the start and take control from the front had reassured the whole squad that their preparations had been spot on. The rowers had nailed the first gold for Team GB just as a few cracks of doubt were beginning to appear in the Olympic edifice. Later that afternoon Bradley Wiggins won a second gold and Britain was away on a glorious, seemingly endless, joyride.

Within the great sweep of Rowing's success, extending in an unbroken line of gold from the 1984 Olympic Games, lay another very human narrative. For 15 years Katherine Grainger had acted as a one-woman snowplough for women's Rowing. A law graduate from Edinburgh University where she had first learnt to row, Grainger had cleared the path for others to follow. She won the first gold at the world Under-23 championships, was part of the first GB women's Eight to win a world championship medal and a member of the women's crew who, moments before the Four took a fifth gold medal for Steve Redgrave at Sydney 2000, had won the first Olympic medal for GB women's Rowing – a silver in the Quadruple Sculls. Her account of the general panic on board during the closing moments of the race was a classic, the subject of raucous laughter around the battered teapot in the old Marlow Boathouse where I first interviewed her.

At the time, she formed a powerful and competitive Pair with Cath Bishop. Between them they could tot up five different degrees, at least one PhD and, mainly due to Cath who is now a high-flying diplomat, five or six languages. However at Athens 2004 Kath and Cath, unable to produce their best form, were beaten to the gold medal by the Romanians. To this day Grainger is not sure whether she was more pleased with winning silver or more disappointed at losing gold, but the significance of the colour really became an issue four years later on a grey day on the Shunyi Park Rowing lake outside Beijing. Widely expected to win the first-ever Great British women's Olympic gold, Grainger and her crew in the Quad Sculls were agonisingly overtaken by the Chinese at the line.

A third silver left Grainger distraught, drained and, as she later admitted, at the lowest ebb in her life. For all her extrovert nature, her easy wit and ready laughter, Grainger reveals little of her real self to the outside world. She has a host of friends in and outside rowing, a strong family and a posse of godchildren, but few people know exactly why she drives herself so hard every hour, every day and in every race. Some of it is due to a Pinsent-like disdain of showing vulnerability, a trait heightened by her role as the mother, the soother of brows, the intercessor, shop steward and leader of the GB women's squad. If there is a problem in the women's group, Katherine will fix it. But she will sort out her own problems in private.

For the year after Beijing 2008, typically, Grainger went away and rowed her own boat, so successfully that she almost scampered away with a gold medal in the women's single sculls at the 2009 world championships. It is possibly the most prized silver medal in her collection. After the race, with her confidence and zest renewed, she knew she would carry on to London 2012. Once she had been paired with Anna Watkins (nee Bebington), a raw but powerful mathematics graduate from Cambridge, she also knew that her best chance of winning that elusive gold had come. Where better to win it than at Eton Dorney, where she had first rowed more than a decade ago?

Only slowly in the build-up to London 2012 did Grainger's quest for gold become a national crusade. She and Watkins form a great double act and, having been unbeaten through three seasons, were hot favourites to win. Yet when their moment of truth came, on Friday 3 August, there was a collective intake of breath at Eton Dorney, in the team hotel and around the country. It lasted until the GB Double Scull crossed the line in style to record the team's second Olympic gold medal and, even more importantly, to bring Grainger her first at the age of 36.

The pair hugged each other in the boat and pretty well everyone else on their return to dry land. Later they enjoyed watching on television the public reaction to their win, a genuine flow of affection for Grainger and for Watkins, who had played her part in the drama to perfection to claim what was also her first gold medal. Only occasionally, if she felt a little sidelined, would Watkins remind an interviewer that it would be her first gold medal too. In the aftermath of their victory, neither would confirm their retirement except, in Grainger's case, to say that if she did continue to 2016 it would only be in the company of her gold medal winning partner.

No one in the GB team was more pleased with the triumphant conclusion to Grainger's golden odyssey than Andrew Triggs Hodge. "I don't know how she found the energy, the mental energy, to keep going,' he said. 'If you bought something made in Britain in the 40s and 50s, it was made to last. That's Katherine.' Some might say the same about Triggs Hodge, but in a different way. After all, he and Peter Reed, the two best oarsmen in the men's squad, had suffered 14 straight defeats at the hands of the brilliant New Zealand pair of Eric Murray and Hamish Bond. Just when they thought they were getting closer, the Kiwis slipped away again. When the British pair were beaten yet again at the 2011 world championships, it was inevitable that they would return to the Four where both had won gold at Beijing 2008. The only problem was that the GB Four, stroked by Alex Gregory, had won the world title in impressive style, asserting their right to be left alone for the Olympic Games. But at the GB trials in April Triggs Hodge and Reed proved their superiority once again, duly joining Gregory and Tom James in the revamped Four for 2012. This was now the flagship GB boat, the golden boat that had not forfeited the Olympic gold medal since the Redgrave Four's historic victory in Sydney. From Redgrave (Sydney 2000) to Pinsent (Sydney 2000, Athens 2004) to Steve Williams (Athens 2004, Beijing 2008) and then Triggs Hodge, Reed and James (all Beijing 2008 and London 2012), the legacy of success has been seamlessly handed down. GB Fours don't lose. But news from the southern hemisphere brought a semblance of reality to the hype. With Drew Ginn, a three-time gold medallist, returning for one last hurrah, Australia were composing a formidable challenge to British hegemony.

The battle lines were drawn at the second World Cup in Lucerne, which brought a morale-boosting win for the British. In Munich a few weeks later, though, came a fearful awakening. Twice the GB Four raced the Australians. Twice they lost, and though it has become a strange tradition that GB crews do not do well in the last competitive regatta before an Olympic Games (the Redgrave Four had finished fourth), the truth hammered home with the subtlety of a blacksmith was that the Australians were a real threat to Triggs Hodge and his men. With the Eight unlikely to beat the Germans and a young pair sure to be outclassed by the New Zealanders, Jurgen Grobler, the Chief Coach for Men, was looking at a surprisingly slender golden thread. With the confidence of one whose crews had won gold at every Olympic regatta (bar the boycott Games of Moscow 1980 and Los Angeles 1984) he knew the Four had natural speed, his numbers told him so. They just needed to find it more regularly and, especially, on the day of the Olympic final.

At a training camp, the first of two before the Olympic Games, the Great Britain crew sat down and tore every-thing apart: attitude, technique, speed, commitment, trust, communication, the whole bag of qualities required to win Olympic gold. 'There was no finger-pointing,' said Triggs Hodge later. 'We sat down, outlined what we wanted to do, how we wanted to do it and why we wanted to do it. We knew the Australians would be pushing us, for sure. So we had to aim for something big.' So they aimed to be two per cent quicker than the rest of the British team, based on times graded for each boat: Single Scull, Pair, Four and Eight. By the end of the first camp in Italy, they had seemingly made little progress; by the end of the sec-ond, in Portugal, they had opened up a margin of one per cent; not enough, but workable. More importantly, the boat was moving fast and the commitment of the crew was unfaltering.

The rowers were starting to think and react as one, to be able to find the speed and to control it, which was the real trick. The opening heat at London 2012 was a breeze, a matter of blowing away cobwebs, but when the GB Four was drawn against the Australians in the semi-final, the psychological warfare began in earnest. Win? Or just qualify for the final with the minimum of effort? Grobler had no doubts. 'We win this,' he told his crew. And win they did, narrowly, but satisfyingly, rowing through the Australian Four in the last 200m. The consensus on the bank was that the Australians were not trying their hardest, but Triggs Hodge and Grobler looked at the video later and saw Ginn lying back in the boat after the line, a surprise from such an experienced oarsman. The GB Four made a point of crossing the line and rowing straight off, without a care in the world. They could catch their breath round the corner out of sight.

Whatever the Australians' reasoning, they had made an error. A day after the semi-final officials finally acknowledged that the wind had switched across the course, which gave a potential advantage to the high-numbered lanes. Instead of being automatically allotted a central lane, the winners of the semi-finals were allowed to pick their final lanes. The British Four chose lane six, furthest away from the grandstands but the best-protected. As losing semi-finalists the Australians were two lanes away, separated from the British by the USA, winners of the other semi-final.

At the back of the boathouse before the race, the crew ran through the strategy with Grobler. The plan was really quite simple: out of the blocks fast, smoothly into transition, push hard to 1500m and let the crowd bring you home. Grobler's final talk is usually a clarion call for courage and effort. This one, Triggs Hodge noted, was more downbeat. His crew did not need any more winding up; just the opposite, they were ready to explode. So Grobler reassured them, calmed them, told them that they had done all this before and that they were ready. Halfway down the course to the start, the GB Four were held under the bridge while a race went past. They saw the Australians, no more than a quick glance. 'Just to check they were all there,' said Triggs Hodge. 'Then it was just us.'

Later, back on the bank, he would describe their race – all six minutes and four seconds of it – as their 'Picasso', their masterpiece. They had never been headed by the Australians, from first stroke to last, and when they reached the last 400m and the cheers rose to a deafening crescendo they forgot about the pain in their legs and their lungs to lift the pace once more. The Australians, who had tried everything to break the British crew, were themselves broken by the combined weight of 25,000 British supporters and a crew of four. By the line, the gap had stretched to more than a second with the USA another two seconds away; they went on to take bronze. It was less Rowing than heavyweight wrestling, I wrote at the time, and it rings as true on reflection as it did then. 'It took huge courage to do that,' said Reed. 'We said what we were going to do and pulled it off.' At the press conference after the race, flanked by his teammates, Ginn spoke of how proud he was to end his career with such a great race against athletes who, he knew, had trained as hard as he had and sacrificed just as much as he had. 'You dig deep inside yourself and you know everyone in these crews has too,' he said. 'It takes a lot to produce what you saw out there.' The gesture was courageous, humbling and poignant, the final dignified testimony of a great Olympic champion who had, at the age of 37, tasted defeat for the first time.

But that was not the end of the medal haul for the British squad, not by a long way. The fuss had barely died down, the Fours had barely vacated the pontoon, when 21-year-old Kat Copeland and 26-year-old Sophie

Hosking, a Durham University chemistry graduate, the dark horses of the whole Siemens-sponsored GB squad, sped down the nearside lane to win Britain's fourth gold in the Lightweight Double Sculls. Though they had only been a partnership for a year, rumours of the women's rapid improvement had emerged from training camp and were immediately confirmed by their performances in the women's earlier rounds. But their innocence still shone through. 'When I crossed the finishing line, I realised it was the Olympic Games,' said a wide-eyed Hosking. They were still trying to grab hold of reality several hours later when the whole team gathered to celebrate at the local pub where Triggs Hodge hung the gold medal round his godmother's neck.

By then, the medal count was official: four golds, two silvers and three bronzes. It was the best in terms of gold since London 1908 and the best-ever overall by a GB Olympic Rowing team. 'I do not think we will be able to do better than this,' said Grobler who, along with Performance Manager David Tanner, has been the architect of the success. Grainger didn't care. For the first time in her life, she felt a deep contentment.

A Triumph of True Grit

Pat Rowley

Team GB's women's Hockey team return from the brink to capture a brilliant bronze

Everyone round the ground heard it: a sickening thud. As the player sank to the ground in agony, it was immediately apparent this was a very serious injury. The captain was down and, in an instant, all the hopes and aspirations of the Great Britain women's Hockey team hung in the balance.

For Kate Walsh was not just the captain. She was the team's outstanding player, the commanding figure, the organiser, the inspiration. Only a few weeks earlier, at the London Cup, we had seen how Team GB struggled without her. Now their talisman was about to leave the biggest stage of all, the London 2012 Olympic Games.

That her jaw was badly fractured was soon apparent; that she would play again in these Olympic Games unthinkable. That she did was amazing, and testament to an extraordinary courage. It was no longer the great player who returned to the Riverbank Arena a few days later, but it was Kate. That was enough to see Great Britain's team on to the podium, collecting the bronze medals and wondering if they might have been of a different hue if the accident had not occurred. Yet in the circumstances, bronze was brilliant. It was Great Britain's first Olympic Hockey medal for 20 years – the first since the women took bronze at the Barcelona 1992 Games.

Britain's men's and women's Hockey teams went to the Games with high hopes, bolstered by successes and a climb up the world rankings. Most critics felt that both sides were capable of making the semi-finals and could, with a little luck, win medals, even gold.

Sacrifices were required to bolster such dreams. Britain's women's team, now ranked fourth in the world, had to accept that they could not take part in the much anticipated Opening Ceremony; their first game was scheduled to take place less than 48 hours later. The Hockey Tournament started at 8.30 am on Sunday 29 July, and it was to prove a long day for Team GB, given a 7pm start for their first game – a huge occasion for many of the team at their first Olympic Games. Most of them had never played in a big stadium filled to capacity and in an electric atmosphere. Even the spectacular blue and pink pitch suddenly seemed alien.

Their first opponents were Japan, ranked ninth, a team Britain had beaten six out of eight times since 1978. Britain had not played them since winning 2–1 at the Beijing 2008 Games. Coach Danny Kerry knew less about them than other teams, and had not been able to prepare as thorough a team plan as he would have wished.

Nervousness showed in the team from the start. Team GB's supporters willed the players to keep the ball as a first priority, to show more composure.

Then Alex Danson seized the moment to do what we all know she can – take advantage of the smallest opening. A little reverse stick push, and there was the ball shooting into goal through the narrowest of spaces between goalkeeper and post. 1–0 to Great Britain after only seven minutes. The goal was greeted with a deafening roar from the flag-waving crowd, and the British players fed off growing excitement in the stands.

The first hurdle had been cleared by half-time, as the marauding side had swept into a 4–0 lead. A quick passing movement had ended with Hannah Macleod, a wound-up clock, cantering into the goalmouth to allow bustling Welshwoman Sarah Thomas to score. Then an even better goal followed. Willowy defender Sally Walton put the finishing touches to a Team GB corner with a confident reverse flick. Finally Danson was fed near goal – something that was not to happen often enough in the tournament – to add the fourth.

In the second half the tally did not increase – it did not need to. Significantly, Japan had not been allowed a single shot on goal.

Then disaster struck. In the closing minutes Kate Walsh, always totally committed, tried to make sure Japan did not have a shot by attempting to tackle from the wrong side. It is always a risky approach, but the 32-year-old captain is known to take that sort of gamble. Earlier this year, in Spain, she had been hit on the head against the USA.

Here the Japanese attacker took a full swing and, as she followed through, her stick smashed against Walsh's unprotected jaw. The crowd gasped and, when the action was shown again on the big screen, they gasped even louder. The whole crowd felt the impact of the blow. Walsh managed to walk off the field clutching ice to her jaw. Taken straight to the medical room, her injury was assessed by various doctors and a dental specialist. It was decided to take her to the London Hospital, where the decision was made to operate the next morning. Any idea of returning to play in this Olympic Games seemed to evaporate with the decision.

The man chosen to do the operation was Simon Holmes, a 48-year-old consultant maxillofacial surgeon. He had been phoned while watching the Team GB Basketball team. 'I met Kate on the Monday morning,' Holmes explained. 'I was immediately most impressed. I can tell you that the pain that she would have experienced at the point of injury would have been demonic.

'I simply asked her three questions. Did she smoke? If she had, then I would have been concerned about infection. How badly did she want to win that medal? How much pain was she prepared to go through?'

'Holmes fitted three plates into Walsh's jaw while his colleague Nayeem Ali made her a face mask. The mask was to give her a psychological edge.'

The consultant surgeon went on to do much more. Having confirmed that the operation went very well, he explained that her jaw would be stronger than it had been. If she recovered from the operation quickly – and she was very fit – he suggested that her Olympic Games might not be over! He gave Walsh the confidence to consider the impossible: that she might yet return to play and see Great Britain to their goal.

Even as the GB team were resigning themselves to being without her, Walsh suddenly had hope. 'There was a job to do. I and my great teammates had spent seven years preparing to win an Olympic gold medal. Provided I didn't disrupt the team, I had to rejoin them.'

Day Three of the tournament started at 8.30am with the Netherlands, the defending champions, having a much tougher time against Japan than had Britain, before taking the match 3–2.

Britain's schedule meant playing every other day, and next up were Korea – a team devastated to lose their opening game 4–0 to China and fighting to survive. From the outset of Britain's afternoon match against these potential semi-finalists, Team GB played nervously. They looked unsettled without Walshie, and with the Koreans denying them any room.

Danson was to change the course of the game. She burst through tackles and set up Nicola White, hardly a recognised goalscorer, to give Britain a lead in the sixth minute. It was ding-dong thereafter. Crista Cullen and Danson scored from British corners and Korea twice came from behind to level at 3–3. With just 13 minutes left on the clock, Britain found that elusive extra gear, snatching late goals by Georgie Twigg and Chloe Rogers in less than a minute for a thrilling 5–3 victory.

That match ended with a fright, too. Danson, Britain's most gifted attacker, rolled an ankle in the last moments and was carried off. Britain's supporters in the stands desperately hoped it was not a serious injury.

At the subsequent press conference, coach Danny Kerry eased our minds about Danson and offered the first glimpse that Walsh was out of the woods. He advised that Walsh had been fitted with a titanium plate – actually three plates, 12 screws and a tie wire. Subject to her reaction to the operation, she might be back in the Olympic Village the next day – with a stronger jaw! He was right. Incredibly Walsh was back the next day, and she even cycled on a treadmill.

On the day of Britain's third match Walsh cycled and had a run. Come evening time there she was, wearing her plastic mask, in the British dug-out.

The game was against Belgium, potentially the easiest

fixture. Great Britain played to their strengths, hounding the Belgians and making space for their attackers. After a lot of unrewarded pressure it was a relief when, just before half-time, Team GB opened the scoring through Ashleigh Ball.

Then Laura Bartlett, one of the two Scots in the team, made it 2–0 early in the second half. Cullen rounded off with a late corner goal. All was going well. Team GB was top of the pool, above Holland on goal difference, with a maximum nine points. Now they were set to meet China, silver medallists at the Beijing 2008 Games. A win or a draw would see Great Britain return to the semi-finals for the first time since 1992.

In the meantime Walshie had progressed to hard run-ning. In the evening before the China match she was back on a pitch with the two nominated reserves, Nat Seymour and Abi Walker. In a demonstration of true team spirit, no one was more supportive of Walsh than Seymour, who could have realised her own Olympic dream by being drafted into the team as replacement for Walsh.

After much heart-searching, the decision was taken to allow Walsh to play against China. The coach sug-gested she be on the bench, but Walsh was adamant. She wanted to be on the field at the start. 'He doesn't usu-ally listen to me,' she told me afterwards, 'but I think he understood that I would know sooner if I was all right.' She could hardly open her mouth, but once she was play-ing, she was quickly taking charge – and talking.

At first Walsh was a shadow of the great player we know. She was extremely tentative in her movements, and the general anxiety spread among the crowd and her players. Meanwhile China, like most Asian women's teams, was too regimented and too defensive. The team were seeking to steal goals, which they duly did from second-half penalty corners through Fu Baorong and Zhao Yudiao. They took two of three chances, and Britain one from five. Cullen's goal came too late, however, and Britain lost 2–1. Cullen summed up their feelings after the game. 'It was unbelievable that Walsh was on the pitch. How could it be that we were not inspired?'

The defeat left Team GB still needing a point to ensure a semi-final place. That would have to come from their final pool match against Holland, the defending champions and world's top-ranked team. It was a big ask.

The first bit of good fortune came before that match. China, the only team that could deny Britain, fell out of the race by losing 1–0 to Japan. Team GB thus went into their last group game against the Netherlands seeking to win by two goals. Such a margin would place them in top place in their pool, allowing them to avoid a semi-final encounter with world champions Argentina.

But the match did not go according to plan. After 19 minutes Danson won Great Britain a corner; Cullen again came up trumps to give the home team a 1–0 half-time lead. It was a start, but a second goal just would not come.

Meanwhile the Dutch, with superior ball skills, waited patiently for openings and duly levelled from a corner. The commanding Maartje Paumen did not unleash her usual devastating flick; she passed instead to the ever-graceful Naomi van As to score. Coach Kerry later complained his side were 'too edgy, too passive'.

In the event the Dutch won 2–1. The decisive goal came because Dutch forward Jonker missed the ball completely when attempting a shot. As Britain's defenders flinched, Kitty van Male was quickest on to the ball. A third goal for Holland was only denied by the impressive Beth Storry, always reliable in the goal.

The Netherlands and Argentina both headed their groups, leaving Britain two days to regroup before meeting Argentina in their semi-final. At least that gave the recovering Walsh, who was looking more assured by the minute, another 48 hours to prepare.

Sadly the semi-final unfolded rather like the Dutch game. The opposition, led by their leggy star player Luciana Aymar, went smoothly about their business, showing excellent close control. Great Britain, never comfortable on the ball, were totally frustrated by Argentina's defence.

Noel Barrionuevo put Argentina ahead from their first corner after five minutes. Carla Rebecchi scored a poacher's goal just before half-time, somehow steering the ball into goal while prostrate in the goalmouth after riding Storry's formidable challenge. Great Britain hardly had a glimpse of a potential goal or the gold medal match until Danson took a half-chance, created by the consistent Helen Richardson. It was enough of a warning for Argentina to shut up shop. This they did with effect.

The Netherlands came through the earlier semi-final against New Zealand only by dominating the first-ever Olympic Hockey penalty shoot-out after a 2–2 draw.

That match confirmed that Britain, after three defeats on the trot, really would have to find their best form to beat the Black Sticks in the bronze medal affray. And they did.

It was very much back to basics. The game plan was good and the British players showed more belief. Admittedly New Zealand, perhaps distracted by the pressure of such a big match, did not do themselves justice. Although often outplayed, they did have two good opportunities to score – one shot rebounding off an upright – and both were missed. Great Britain made their opponents pay by excellent corner drills. Walsh came forward to join Cullen at the top of the circle for the set-pieces. Her passes produced two goals, scored by Danson and Thomas. Cullen flicked home with uncanny accuracy in between, finishing her Olympic Games as joint top scorer with Danson, at five goals apiece. That didn't alter the fact that the bedrock of Britain's success was the defence of Storry, Unsworth, Walsh, Cullen and the second Scot, Maguire.

The last minutes of the match were a crescendo of jubilation. Everyone was counting down the time long before Michelsen did score from a Black Sticks corner, and that proved too late to change the result. Celebrations were soon in full swing, and the players were even joined by another Kate, HRH The Duchess of Cambridge. A player in her schooldays, she has shown more than a passing interest in the team for some time and helped to bring the game much valuable publicity.

'We were heartbroken after our semi-final,' Walsh reflected. 'Devastated. People couldn't talk. All we had dreamed of was gold. When we knew the gold had gone, we vowed we weren't going to go home empty-handed. We knew that we had the game. We knew that we had the mental capacity. We just had to put it all together.'

Netherlands beat Argentina 2–0 in a quality gold medal match, with their men's team, who lost 2–1 to Germany in their final, coming so close to being the first country to achieve an Olympic Hockey double. But for Team GB's women, the bronze medal, in such circumstances, was a magnificent achievement. When Walsh received her medal, the roar said it all. Little did the crowd know just how great her courage had been.

Let surgeon Simon Holmes, the person who best knew what Walsh had endured, have the last word:

'In order to get her to play on the Saturday, we needed

three weeks healing in three days. The fracture came together well, but the rest was down to her.

'I have treated very many facial trauma patients, the great and good of the East End, including some very, very hard men. Not one can hold a candle up to her for bravery in facing her injury and immediate recovery.

'Watching her play really filled me with a mixture of anxiety and pride. The deal was that if she broke it again we could have mended her again, but that would have been it. I am not sure I could have watched her defend a rising shot at a penalty corner!

'Seeing Britain win those medals justified it all. Sure, I had to push Kate psychologically, but I just had this feeling that she would pull it off. A lady of true grit.'

All's Well that Ends Well

Kate Battersby

*Aileen McGlynn and her new pilot overcome
disappointment to relish two hard-won Paralympic medals*

Aileen McGlynn sat on a chair in the middle of the
Olympic Velodrome, her eyes closed, her head resting on
the wall behind her. The tumult of the 6,000-strong home
crowd was bouncing off the walls in the magnificent new
facility, but from her place on the infield McGlynn didn't
want to hear it. The extraordinary sound should have signalled her third straight Paralympic gold medal in her
specialist event, and her fourth career Paralympic gold in
all. Twice previously, at Athens 2004 and Beijing 2008,
she had entered the 1km Time Trial – B event for blind
and partially sighted cyclists, and twice previously she had
scorched to victory over that time trial. She had made the
1km Time Trial – B her event, and had no experience of
anything other than triumph in it at the Paralympic Games.

All that had now changed. At London 2012, her home
Games, she and Helen Scott, her sighted pilot in the tandem events since mid-2011, had fallen short. The crowd
generously acknowledged the victors – McGlynn's old
rival, Australia's Felicity Johnson, and her pilot Stephanie
Morton – as they took their lap of honour. At every stage
of their ride the Australians had been ahead of schedule.

They had not only surged to victory, but had also broken the Paralympic record McGlynn had set with her former pilot Ellen Hunter at Beijing 2008. On the Velodrome's super-fast track, so similar in design to that used by the Great British squad in their Paralympic training camp in Newport, McGlynn and Scott had been left more than half a second adrift.

McGlynn struggled to accept the thought. She didn't want to take it in, even though logic told her that her partnership with Scott, barely a year old, was still in its infancy. The five-year career she shared with Hunter was littered with championship golds set in world record time, and it was too much to expect to match those heights so soon with Scott. McGlynn could take some comfort from the fact that she and Scott had set a new personal best time of 1:09.469 in the final. Of course she had known the Australians were favourites, ever since they had broken McGlynn's world record in Los Angeles in February 2012, on their way to winning the world title. Taking silver there behind Johnson had only sharpened McGlynn's unflagging determination. 'Second place is not good enough,' she would say relentlessly to interviewers. 'I don't like losing.'

The 39-year-old Glaswegian had come to London 2012 hungry for more golds. Silver in her specialist event, the 1km Time Trial – B, was not the response she wanted, but silver was what she had won. Many times McGlynn had experienced post-race exhaustion in victory; now the same exhaustion in defeat punched home her sense of loss. Alone in her chair, fatigue and disappointment were scored into her face.

McGlynn felt a hand on her shoulder. It was Helen Scott, smiling broadly – at 22, attending her first Paralympic

Games, she found it hard not to be thrilled with silver. For her it was simpler to quash any disappointment with the thought that in producing a personal best on the biggest stage, they could have done no more. McGlynn stood up, returning the smile, and hugged her Cycling partner. Anyone looking at them in that moment could have been fooled into thinking McGlynn was content with the outcome, when in truth she had never felt lower. All that work, all that anticipation of her home Games – for silver.

And yet … life turns in mysterious ways. Two days later the pair would take bronze in the Pursuit – B – and McGlynn would be utterly elated, declaring London 2012 to be one of the best experiences of her life. In those moments after the 1km Time Trial – B silver, the idea of being delighted by bronze in the Pursuit – B would have seemed nonsense to McGlynn. Hers has been a life of many journeys; but for all its brevity, the two-day journey she travelled between the 1km Time Trial – B and the Pursuit – B was the most unexpected of all.

Born in Glasgow in June 1973, McGlynn had from childhood never given much thought to being partially sighted. It seemed normal to her, especially as her two sisters had the same condition. At six, young Aileen discovered that it made scant difference to her ability to ride a bike – so much so that when she joined a cycling club at 14 she saw no reason to mention her sight, leaving it to her Johnstone Wheelers clubmates to work out the situation. As far as she was concerned, there was nothing to tell.

It took time for McGlynn to become a full-time athlete – she was 31 before she attended her debut Paralympic Games. She studied for a degree in mathematics, statistics and management science at the University of Strathclyde, and became a trainee actuary (a statistician computing insurance risks and premiums), but cycling was on her mind too much of the time.

Like all blind and visually impaired cyclists, McGlynn competed on a fixed-wheel tandem. She would team up with a sighted partner to be her 'pilot' on the front seat, while she as 'stoker' provided the engine power on the back. The partnership was critical, and finding one that could perform magically together did not happen over-night. Only when McGlynn hooked up with Ellen Hunter after the turn of the millennium did she begin to win the really big prizes. Hunter herself had been on something of a journey. In 2003, the year before the Athens 2004 Paralympic Games, the Wrexham cyclist broke her back during a race in Kent, to be told she might never cycle again. She emerged after six weeks in hospital deter-mined to be a better and stronger cyclist than ever.

Together McGlynn and Hunter became all but invinci-ble. At Athens 2004 they won gold in the 1km Time Trial – B 1–3 and silver in the Sprint – B 1–3. Four years later at Beijing 2008 they did better still, repeating their gold in the 1km Time Trial – B & V1 1–3 before claiming the ulti-mate prize in the Pursuit – B & V1 1–3. Both women were awarded the OBE in the New Year's Honours List of 2009. But when the pair fell short of a medal at the world cham-pionships in Manchester that year Hunter, at the age of 41, felt the time was right to retire.

Finding another harmonious tandem partner for McGlynn was not a swift process. No one has very clear ideas on what creates the elusive synchronicity necessary for a good pairing. There is a curious dynamic to the tandem, not least through the simplistic theory that two on a bike automatically generate as much speed as a solo rider. In fact the extra weight brings potential instability, and when fatigue sets in it has an impact on speed.

Creating a successful new pair largely comes down to trial and error, and it was not until 2011 that McGlynn cemented a partnership with Helen Scott. The (then) 21-year-old had been a dedicated cyclist since the age of ten, and her dream was to be a professional. She was accepted on to the British Cycling programme in 2008, where the training did not suit her. However, the head coach of the national British para-cycling squad spotted her potential as a pilot. Scott loved the new venture so much that she has vowed never to return to the able-bodied version of the sport. Moreover, she and McGlynn gelled so fast that they won three silver medals at the 2012 world championships. Both knew the real target was the London 2012 Paralympic Games, where the programme permitted them to enter just two events.

The first was the 1km Time Trial – B on Friday 31 August, day two of the Games. McGlynn and Scott were drawn to ride second last, leaving only Felicity Johnson and Stephanie Morton to go afterwards. The British women waited in the infield while others took their turn, focusing only on themselves, placing all their competitive energy into what was to come. Then they were called to the start line and Scott, mouth dry, led the two of them out to the track where British coaches were waiting with their carbon-framed tandem. The crowd noise, now a part of sporting legend at London 2012, crashed in waves around them. All their training had been for this moment.

As ever in a tandem event, the start was particularly crucial. McGlynn and Scott nailed it, overcoming the difficulty of pulling together, the line of the bike straight, their shoulders in unison, with no rocking between pilot and stoker, the bike moving as one. With half a lap out of four done, they were already an extraordinary 1.390 up on the previous best time set by Phillipa Gray and Laura Thompson of New Zealand. As they gathered pace, McGlynn's stillness as stoker was vital if Scott was to control the path of the tandem at speed and hold the racing line. At 250m, their advantage was more than two seconds. But the early investment of energy could not be sustained. They finished 1.776 up on the New Zealand pair, having never gone faster in their year together. But it was down on the time that McGlynn and Hunter set at Beijing 2008.

McGlynn knew a time below one minute and nine seconds would be required to give them a chance of gold. She feared their time of 1:09.469 would not be enough, and she was right. Disappointment enveloped her as she sat alone on the infield, her eyes closed, her head resting on the wall behind her. Minutes later live television microphones were pointing her way.

'It would have been nice to win gold,' said McGlynn with a shrug. 'We came out well and really went for it, but it just didn't happen for us on the day. We're really pleased to have got a silver and to do a PB as a team was really good. The atmosphere was amazing. The home support was a massive help.'

She was glad when the microphones pointed somewhere else. After the Victory Ceremony McGlynn went into the stands to watch her teammates in their races. She wanted to escape from the all-seeing eyes of the television cameras, and to be simply anonymous among a crowd.

And that was when something wonderful happened. The crowd would not let her be anonymous. Immediately spotting her signature blonde hair, they had only acclaim for their heroine. Supporters clustered round to tell McGlynn of their pride in her, to thank her for all the thrills she had given them. They queued to have their photograph taken with her, and could not contain their delight at being permitted to touch the talismanic medal around her neck. McGlynn began to see her achievement at one remove from the competitive bubble that was her norm. And suddenly her world was a different place.

Abruptly the thought of her second event, the Pursuit – B in two days' time, filled her with excitement. It did not matter that the 1km Time Trial – B, her specialist event, was behind her. It did not matter that she and Scott had barely done any specific pursuit training since May. Another medal was possible. Another medal was what she wanted. And she was going to get it.

Sunday 2 September arrived. The Pursuit – B would require two races of McGlynn and Scott, with the fastest riders from a series of heats going through to two ride-offs, one to decide gold and the other bronze. McGlynn and Scott won their heat with ease, posting a time less than one-tenth outside McGlynn's 2008 Paralympic record. But then came one of those astonishing moments which occasionally happen in elite sport. The New Zealand pair of Gray and Thompson – bronze medallists in the 1km Time Trial – B, but unfancied in this event – not only broke the world record of eight years' standing in their heat, but sliced almost five seconds off it. Moreover, they towed the pair they beat – Ireland's world champions Catherine Walsh and Fran Meehan – to a faster time than McGlynn and Scott, demoting them from the gold medal decider. Instead they would race off for bronze against their fellow Britons, Lora Turnham and Fiona Duncan. A great contest was brewing, with the Paralympic debutante Turnham, set against the old hand McGlynn.

Four hours after the morning heats, the two British pairs

lined up on the track. The crowd, thrilled by the certainty of a domestic medal, hardly knew which bike to cheer for. Early on McGlynn and Scott took half a second's advantage, but one kilometre into the 3,000 metre race saw Turnham edging ahead. With two-thirds of the race completed, there was still just a tenth of a second in the younger woman's favour. With 750 metres to go, however, experience began to tell. At the bell McGlynn's lead was six-tenths of a second, and by the finish it had stretched to more than a second. The crowd was delirious as McGlynn and Scott circled the track. It was not gold. It was not even silver. But McGlynn had never known a feeling like it. 'To come out and pip them for bronze – we're so chuffed,' grinned McGlynn afterwards. 'It's better than winning the silver in the Time Trial. We knew Lora and Fiona would really give us a fight. The Pursuit – B is their event, and we only qualified for the race-off one-tenth faster than them.'

'We came to ride in two events, and have medalled in both,' teammate Scott added happily. 'The only thing better would have been two golds. It means we have unfinished tandem business now and want to complete our set of medals at Rio in 2016.'

McGlynn agreed. The woman who just two days previously was overwhelmed with disappointment at silver could not have been more enchanted by bronze. 'The crowd has been amazing," she explained. 'After winning my silver medal I went up into the stands for a while and everybody was so pleased … I'd like to thank everyone who came up and asked me for my photograph. This has been an absolutely amazing experience because of them.' McGlynn's third Paralympic Games had delivered her not only two further medals, but also a feeling of deep content.

A World Turned Upside Down

Pippa Cuckson

Great Britain's horses and riders triumph in the magnificent Greenwich Park

The delighted punch in the air as he powered through the finish meant much to Peter Charles. He had just secured Britain's first Jumping Team Competition gold in the Olympic Games since Helsinki 1952, and in the most challenging of circumstances – a round where time both raced and stood heart-stoppingly still. Yet for Charles it was just as important to be the rider who made a difference, who delivered a dramatic victory, after his nightmare start to London 2012.

Charles, a former European champion, is no stranger to the big time, but, at nine years old, his horse Vindicat was inexperienced. He froze with fear at his first sight of the Greenwich Park arena and its excitable capacity crowd of 23,000. Then he spooked himself, never mind his supporters, when he crashed through the third jump of the opening Individual qualifier, immune to his rider's reassuring commands. Team manager Rob Hoekstra hastily changed tactics, deciding to run the three stronger combinations – Nick Skelton (Big Star), Ben Maher (Tripple X) and Scott Brash (Hello Sanctos) – first in the next day's critical Team contest. He hoped they would build up enough of a lead to discard Charles's score if necessary.

The ploy worked, and as the two-day, two-round Team event progressed Britain seemed on target. Big Star lived up to popular billing as 'best show jumper in the world' with two flawless rounds. But in horse sport you must expect the unexpected, and a late run by the Netherlands left them tying with Britain for gold. To everyone's surprise, all four riders found themselves being instructed to jump off against the clock. Suddenly, the Equestrian equivalent of a penalty shoot-out was relying on Vindicat, Great Britain's weakest link, to kick the deciding ball.

Skelton set the pace, and Maher and Brash wore down the Dutch team, but aggregated times were as important as fences down. 'I could hardly bear it,' said Skelton. 'Riding all four rounds myself would have seemed preferable to watching!' It seemed inconceivable that Charles could overcome Vindicat's nerves and transmit to his horse that this was no ordinary day at the office. Yet his control held steady. Vindicat remained calm and the pair clinched victory. Their gutsy run left the entire UK horse community, glued to television screens in offices and stable yards, collectively holding its breath. Sport lovers everywhere joined them, poised in expectation. Charles nearly burst with pride. 'I wasn't much use for the rest of the week, but I did come good in the end,' he said.

The British team that last won Olympic gold 60 years ago at Helsinki 1952 included Harry Llewellyn and Foxhunter, founding fathers of the modern sport. At 54, and returning to top level after breaking his neck, Skelton is a legend himself, but even he had to wait until his sixth Games to win an Olympic medal. Normally undemonstrative, Skelton was overwhelmed, hugging a surprised Clare Balding of the BBC on air and leading a long night's partying at the Greenwich Tavern – a pub now renamed The Gold and Saddle in honour of its fortnight as the horse world's adopted watering hole.

Skelton was soon back to business. The defending Individual Jumping Competition champion, Eric Lamaze of Canada, had tipped Skelton to succeed him. Yet in a cruel twist Big Star, the horse that jumped more rounds and accrued fewer faults than any other throughout the week, was to be denied a second medal. The Olympic format restarts individuals on a clean sheet, discounting achievements thus far. Contenders had to jump two massive tracks, and as the contest closed Skelton was still up there, expecting to jump off for gold against Switzerland's Steve Guerdat on Nino de Buissonets. Skelton's every move was accompanied by appreciative gasps from the stands, but when Big Star rolled a rail three from home, his first major-event error in three years, that dream came to an end.

The tussle was then for Individual silver, between Gerco Schroeder of the Netherlands (on a horse deliberately named London) and the eventual bronze medallist, Ireland's Cian O'Connor (Blue Loyd) – an astonishing case of being in the right place at the right time. O'Connor had accrued 12 faults in the week's earlier rounds and did not initially qualify. He was admitted to the Individual Competition just two hours before the event, when Casall, the horse of European champion Rolf-Goran Bengtsson, failed the final veterinary check. Grasping his chance, O'Connor jumped cleanly, dropping just one time-penalty across the first two legs. The rider attributed his success to his 'never say never' approach. 'I am not the greatest rider in the world, but I am the most organised,' he said. 'I kept preparing Blue Loyd as if he was to jump another day.'

The week's main talking point was the capitulation

of show jumping powerhouses Germany, France and Belgium in the Team Competition, and the bronze claimed by a startled Saudi Arabian quartet, Prince Abdullah Al Saud, Ramzy Al Duhami, Kamal Bahamdan and Abdullah Al Sharbatly, who have an average world ranking of just 182. At the halfway stage they even led, and held most of their nerves overnight to retain a podium place. Saudi Arabia is a 'young' equestrian country, but a wealthy one. It fast-tracked riders into the global elite with a £40 million investment in ready-made Grand Prix jumpers, making irresistible offers to individual owners in rival countries, including Britain. They backed up the strategy by pre-selecting a sextet three years ago and basing them in Belgium, accompanied by Olympian Stanny van Paesschen. He has honed the horses into a highly effective unit, establishing a formula that may well now appeal to other new jumping entrants.

Any medal in Jumping was a bonus, though some may think Great Britain was short-changed at the start of the Olympic fortnight in the Eventing; Britain propagated this all-round horseman's discipline, after all.

There was an extra, inevitable pressure on the British Eventing team for it included HM The Queen's granddaughter, Zara Phillips. A former world and European champion, Phillips is well used to an accompanying media circus, but her stoic attempts to point out she was only one of five key riders invariably failed. 'Can the bloke stand in the middle?' demanded photographers at the Eventing competition photo-call. The 'bloke' – reigning world silver medallist, world number one ranked rider and six-times winner of Burghley, William Fox-Pitt – uncomplainingly obliged.

On Eventing cross-country day, organisers pulled off ambitious plans to admit 50,000 spectators to the limited and hilly 5.7 km course set out over Greenwich Park – the one Equestrian competition not staged entirely in the temporary arena. No one seemed to mind not being able to get an unencumbered view at every fence. Fans were just thrilled to be at London 2012, and their non-stop cheering meant horses confronted an unfamiliar corridor of sound all around the Park. This unprecedented interest had one unexpected disadvantage for riders. They were unable to hear their stopwatches 'bleep' at the minute-markers, essential for finishing the course on time.

Greenwich, initially a controversial venue choice, magnificently delivered LOCOG's vision of bringing Equestrian events to the heart of the city. At most post-war Games they have invariably been staged an hour or so out of town – at Melbourne 1956 (Stockholm) and Beijing 2008 (Hong Kong) they were held in a different country. The backdrop of Canary Wharf, the historic Queen's House and the National Maritime Museum combined the innovation and tradition associated with England's vibrant capital city.

Eventing was to be Germany's day. For generations cross-country riding had been Germany's bête noir, but, weaned off a forensic riding style by British coach Christopher Bartle, the country had taken an unexpected gold at Beijing 2008. Now Michael Jung was set to become the first rider to hold world, European and Olympic titles simultaneously, while securing Germany's second consecutive gold. Jung and the peerless Sam usually lead from the start, but this time teammate Ingrid Klimke (Butts Abraxxas) and Sweden's Sara Algotsson-Ostholt (Wega) jointly topped the opening dressage phase. Jung quietly worked his way up the order on cross-country, securing the Individual gold with two polished jumping rounds.

Cross-country day produced the proverbial afternoon

of thrills and spills, the terrain and tight turns proving every bit as challenging as the 30 jumps. The helter-skelter course was never going to play to the strengths of British riders, brought up on the galloping, open parkland tradition of Badminton and Burghley. Zara Phillips' fast round on High Kingdom momentarily put Great Britain in gold medal position, but by close of play they were back in silver, with Mary King – at 51 the oldest female in Team GB – and 2008 dual bronze medallist Tina Cook both in sight of the Individual podium.

High Kingdom was one of 10 horses to lose their metal shoes on the course. The grass footing was newly planted, so many riders applied extra-long anti-slip studs, at the increased risk of levering the whole shoe off at 25 miles an hour. High Kingdom inevitably felt his feet on the final day and lowered two jumps in the decider. Tabloids may have reported that Zara Phillips had 'lost Britain the gold', but those familiar with the nuances of eventing recognised she had in reality secured Team silver. The fast-improving New Zealand squad, including two seven-time Olympians Mark Todd and Andrew Nicholson, moved into bronze.

The Eventing was an emotional rollercoaster, especially so for two riders. Algotsson-Ostholt thought she had jumped clean to take the Individual gold, but tapped the final rail. It fell so belatedly that the rider's squeal of joy dramatically changed to a wail of despair when she heard it plop on to the sand. She took the Individual silver, ahead of Sandra Auffarth (Opgun Luovo), who secured bronze for Germany. The Olympic Games' unusual format requirement for riders to jump twice was a round too far for Cook and King. Poor Yoshi Oiwa of Japan made history as the first Asian rider to lead the dressage phase at any eventing championship, only to spill over on the flat

– not even when attempting a jump – on cross-country.

Fox-Pitt had qualified 10 horses for London 2012, but was convinced Lionheart was the one most likely to 'ping' round Greenwich Park. He found out the hard way that Greenwich did not suit him at all, but he still relished the ride. 'It was a wonderful, once-in-a-lifetime venue. We won't see anything like it in our sport again. Winning double gold at Rio de Janeiro could not compare with the London experience,' Fox-Pitt said.

Staging the Equestrian events in an accessible central venue attracted a large contingent of non-specialist media who struggled to decipher the difference between the three medal disciplines. The penny dropped when the purist Dressage trio of Charlotte Dujardin (riding Valegro), Carl Hester (Uthopia) and Laura Bechtolsheimer (Mistral Hojris) took to the stage. The telepathic ease with which they charmed their horses into pirouette, passage (the 'slow motion' trot) and tempi-changes (the equine skip) garnered two further gold medals and a bronze for Team GB. It also delivered the popular new moniker of 'horse dancing' for this most esoteric of skills.

That Britain was even entering London 2012 as Dressage favourite seemed inconceivable back at Athens 2004; a post-war period dominated by Germany and the Netherlands had seen dressage become the 'poor relation' of British equestrianism. Great Britain had won occasional minor medals at European level, but its heady rise began only after Beijing 2008. It was brought about first by private investors, prepared to remain for the long haul – in the case of training a Dressage medallist, six years – so that riding talent could be paired with the right calibre of horse. It then needed the willingness of such investors to resist the multi-million pound offers for the finished article, at least until the week after London 2012. The third factor was the foresight of Hester himself who, spotting Dujardin as his most gifted student in 20 years, decided in 2007 to lend her Valegro, then just a work-in-progress.

Britain won its first Team gold at the European championships of 2011. Dujardin, who was in the team at Rotterdam, had then been competing at this level for just eight months. A year later she had smashed a world record score and was about to create two new Olympic ones. Yet nothing was certain. London 2012 was a big challenge for any team; an electric atmosphere presented the danger of horses 'blowing up' at any moment, and there was also a change of format to contend with, the Team medal now being decided by two separate set tests. A new-look, all-female German squad, Helen Langehanenberg, Kristina Sprehe and Dorothee Schneider, gave Great Britain a tougher run than expected, only 0.5 per cent behind after the completion of the Grand Prix. 'There was then a three-day wait for the Grand Prix Special; sticking to the horses' normal routine was the really difficult thing,' recalls Hester. 'We had to keep them interested while not over-training them to the extent we put them off Dressage. It was especially odd for our horses, as they are used to going out in their fields.' But the British trio held on for a historic Team gold. As Hester told Dujardin when she entered the field of play, 'Some people wish it would happen; some people hope it will happen; you're going to make it happen!'

When the rider is not the owner, the heartbreak of being 'jocked-off' a top horse is never far away. Such a situation lay behind the appreciative, non-partisan cheer by the crowd at Greenwich Park for Edward Gal of the Netherlands. This world champion had raised the bar worldwide with Totilas, only for the super-stallion to be controversially sold against his will to a German buyer 18 months before the Games. Gal's new equine partner Undercover, although not Totilas, helped the Netherlands to take Team bronze, alongside Adelinde Cornelissen (Parzival), then the world-number-one-ranked rider, and three-time Olympic champion Anky van Grunsven (Salinero), whose Olympic medal tally of nine became an Equestrian record.

Shining star Dujardin brought the capacity crowd to its feet for a second time when securing Individual gold on the last day at Greenwich to a medley of patriotic themes, including *The Great Escape*, James Bond 007 and the chimes of Big Ben. A set-test result is no true barometer for the freestyle, and European and World Cup champion Cornelissen looked the winner. Dujardin thought so, too, and was anticipating silver ahead of Bechtolsheimer's certain bronze until the result came over the public address system. As the roar of approval reverberated across the Thames, Dujardin broke down in tears. The Olympic debutante is only the fourth female British athlete from any sport to win two gold medals at a single Games.

As the Olympic Games drew to a close, Federation Equestre International eventing Chairman Giuseppe Della Chiesa succinctly summed up an extraordinary 12 days. 'Two golds for Germany in Eventing, two golds for Britain in Dressage – the world has turned upside down!'

'It's surpassed any dream I ever imagined …
I will always remember that last 100m of the
800m, running down the home straight, the
roar of the crowd. It was pretty special.'

Jessica Ennis, Heptathlon gold medallist

7
GOLDEN GLORIES

Sheffield Steel Turns to Gold

Vikki Orvice

*Jessica Ennis storms to Heptathlon success
on 'Super Saturday'*

It was as if the perfect script had been written. Jessica Ennis, her arms outstretched, crosses the finishing line in the Olympic Stadium to win gold at the London 2012 Games.

For Ennis hails from Sheffield, the city where the London Organising Committee for the Olympic and Paralympic Games Chair Lord Coe told International Olympic Committee (IOC) delegates he had been inspired to pursue a career in athletics when, as a schoolboy, he watched local hero John Sherwood win a bronze medal at the Mexico City 1968 Games. Coe's thought-provoking and inspirational presentation to IOC delegates in Singapore in 2005 helped London to win the bid for the 2012 Games and coined the slogan 'Inspire a Generation', which was plastered on posters across the Olympic Park and at venues throughout the country over the course of the Games.

On Saturday 4 August 2012, just after 8.35pm on a warm summer evening, Ennis crossed the finishing line of the 800m to win Heptathlon gold with a personal best and national record of 6,955 points. In doing so she inspired young and old among the 80,000 spectators lucky enough to have a ticket to the Olympic Stadium, as well as countless millions watching on television sets around the world.

Days before the Opening Ceremony, as she prepared at a British team training camp in Portugal for the biggest weekend of her life, Ennis had pledged to be part of a Golden Hour of Athletics in the Olympic Stadium. In the event it turned out to be a golden 44 minutes as Ennis's success in the Heptathlon was quickly followed by Olympic golds for Greg Rutherford in the Long Jump and Mo Farah in the 10,000m, on what was one of the greatest nights ever witnessed in British Athletics.

Ennis was the first Briton to win an Athletics gold medal at a London Games since 1908. Her total tally was just 45 points short of the magic 7,000 Heptathlon mark that only four women in history have ever achieved, and only one at an Olympic Games – world record holder Jackie Joyner-Kersee (USA). A mark that is viewed in multi-eventing as equal to the four-minute-mile barrier.

In scenes reminiscent of the night local heroine Cathy Freeman won 400m gold at the Sydney 2000 Games, hundreds of flashbulbs went off around the Olympic Stadium in London as Ennis took to the track for the final element of the seven-event competition. The 800m. She could almost have jogged the two laps, such was the margin of victory she already had over her rivals – including Russian Federation athlete Tatyana Chernova, the woman who had taken the world title from her in Daegu a year earlier. Instead Ennis went into the lead at the bell, only to lose it again before doing what every true champion does. Finish in style: storm down the back straight with the crowd going wild, the crescendo of noise drowning out the beat from Massive Attack's *Unfinished Sympathy* over the PA system.

There was nothing left unfinished for 26-year-old Ennis, no sympathy required. She had finally achieved her dream of Olympic gold in arguably the toughest female discipline in track and field sport. The Olympic motto of 'Faster, Higher, Stronger' was exemplified by her every move over the two days of competition.

Such was the measure of her performance that she crushed defending Olympic champion Nataliya Dobrynska, who took the world indoor crown from Ennis in March but was forced to drop out injured after the long jump. Second to Ennis was the German Lilli Schwarzkopf, with Chernova having to settle for bronze after finishing 327 points behind the 5ft 4in British athlete.

Then came the tears, a rare show of public emotion from the girl with nerves of Sheffield Steel, as she draped a Union flag around her shoulders for the lap of honour with the rest of the Heptathlon field. By the time she stood on top of the podium to receive the gold medal from Sir Craig Reedie, who as former chairman of the British Olympic Association was one of the first to have the idea that London should bid for these Games as early as 1997, and a bouquet from none other than Coe himself, she was smiling again.

'I'm usually quite reserved,' Ennis admitted. 'I might do a little clap and that's as excited as I get. I never cry, well not in public anyway. I was so overwhelmed and emotional, I couldn't hold it back. A once-in-a-lifetime opportunity could have been lost, gone forever, and I can't believe I took it. Seb Coe presented me with my silver medal in Daegu in Korea in 2011. He was very excited and said it was very different with the gold this time. He was really proud. They were the best moments, crossing the line and being on the podium.'

Ennis had been helped on by that crowd of 80,000 at the Olympic Stadium from the moment she stepped on to the track for her opening event, the 100m hurdles, on the morning of Friday 3 August 2012. She ran the race in the fastest-ever time by a heptathlete, setting a new British record of 12.54 – exactly the same time as American Dawn Harper's winning performance in the individual 100m Hurdles at the Beijing 2008 Games.

Such crowd numbers for a morning session are unheard-of at major championships. Among those in the stands who realised they were witnessing something special were her fiancé Andy, a construction worker who she first met at school, mum Alison, a social worker, dad Vinnie, a painter and decorator, and sister Carmel, who works as a nursery nurse.

Jessica tried to explain the effect the crowd had on her. 'I couldn't imagine how the crowd would lift me until I was actually there. I kind of expected it to be a bit empty as well. I'd only been to world championships and it's always a bit empty in the morning. When I first stepped into the Stadium that Friday morning I couldn't believe it. It just gave me goosebumps. My coach, Toni Minichiello, told me "You have 80,000 friends out there." He kept saying it before every event. I could tell my mum was stressed before I competed. She went to the Opening Ceremony, saw the crowd there and kept saying don't be overwhelmed, the crowd will be big. Apparently they were all in the third row back when I did the long jump and they moved further back so I couldn't see them and get distracted.'

The long jump. Having gone into the second day of competition with an overnight lead of 184 points over Lithuania's Austra Skujyte she had to make sure there was no repeat of the errors in recent long jump competitions.

Ennis had struggled with her long jump all season until the multi-event meeting in the Austrian village of Götzis in May, where she equalled her personal best of 6.51m en route to breaking Denise Lewis' 12-year-old British record. That record was set just months before Lewis won Heptathlon gold in Sydney, inspiring the teenage Ennis back home in Sheffield.

After a poor opening jump of 5.95m, which set alarm bells ringing, Ennis recovered to produce a leap of 6.48m in her third and final effort, to gain a huge tally of 1001 points. The relief on her face was clear to see. 'I knew I had nailed it then,' she explained. 'I knew I was pretty much on my way to gold because my javelin had been going well in training, but I was worried about the long jump because it had been pretty much up and down all year. I kept thinking, "Am I going to throw it all away doing three no jumps?" So it was a massive relief to have got that right. To have got a solid jump and then a personal best in the javelin was more than I could have asked for.'

Yes, a personal best in the javelin.

Her javelin had let her down at the 2011 World Athletics Championships in Daegu, when she was forced to hand over the title she had won in Berlin in 2009 to Chernova and settle for silver. Under the guidance of former javelin thrower Mick Hill her form improved, and she set a personal best of 47.11m in Götzis. At London she even bettered that, throwing a lifetime best of 47.49m, worth 812 points.

Among those watching in the Olympic Stadium for the morning session on 5 August 2012 was Sheffield pop star Jarvis Cocker, whose band Pulp famously sang *Do You Remember the First Time?* Ennis certainly will, having never even competed in London before, let alone at the Olympic Games. She first took up athletics when she was sent to an event for children in the school holidays at Sheffield's Don Valley Stadium. Her mum always jokes that it had simply been to provide some cheap childcare. Instead it paved the way for an Olympic champion. When the news broke in July 2005 that London had won the 2012 Games, Ennis was a psychology student at Sheffield University. Three weeks after the Singapore decision, she became the first Briton to win Heptathlon gold at the European Junior Championships. Expectations were beginning to build.

Bronze was to follow at the Commonwealth Games in 2006, but on the eve of the Beijing 2008 Games she suffered a career-threatening foot injury and was forced to miss out. As Ennis now realises, it just wasn't her time. 'I kind of had a feeling it was meant to be in London. I do believe things happen for a reason, and this was supposed to be my path to London. If I had gone to Beijing and won a medal I might not have even been competing at London 2012.'

This feeling that she had a date with destiny buoyed Ennis up throughout the London 2012 Games. 'I could hear the noise of the crowd when I was just about to come out into the Olympic Stadium on Friday morning, but what was weird is how calm I felt. I had felt nervous a couple of days before, but once I got to the Stadium I was ready. When I stepped out the noise gave me such a lift. It was brilliant. I just loved it. I stayed at the Stadium on Saturday between sessions. Seven hours to kill before the 800m, the final event. I listened to Massive Atttack over and over again on my iPod, trying to switch off, but it was so hard. My mind was all over the place. I kept thinking about crossing the line and winning gold and how I would feel, then I thought what if I fall over. Mick (Hill) was saying "You've done it, you've done it", but I told him I still had one event left and I've got to plan the race. What was really strange is that while I was waiting to come out for my 800m I could hear the stadium DJ playing Massive Attack for the previous race.'

Having won the race in unforgettable style, Ennis described 'coming down' afterwards. 'When I got back to the Olympic Village on Saturday night after seeing my family and Andy it was very late, about three in the morning. We all had apartments and there were seven athletes in ours. On my door were little notes from Goldie Sayers, Yamilé Aldama, Lee McConnell and Nicola Sanders congratulating me. One said: "You made me cry". They were all asleep, so I had to creep in and be really quiet. I didn't wake anyone up because obviously they were still competing but it was lovely to see the notes on the door.'

And then came the realisation that her life had changed forever. 'I had my medal beside me for my two hours of sleep. When I woke up I just looked at it. I felt disbelief more than anything. I couldn't believe I had done it. I dreamed of this as a kid, but it's so much better. It's surpassed any dream I ever imagined. My name is in the Olympic history books. As a young athlete that's one thing I always said that I wanted, for people to remember my name as a great athlete. I've done that now. I will always remember that last 100m of the 800m, running down the home straight, the roar of the crowd. It was pretty special. Hopefully we can now inspire a new generation and it will have a knock-on effect for the next few years.'

Winning Wheels Keep Rolling

Gareth A Davies

The 'Tough of the Track' turns home turf to gold – four times

By Sunday 9 September, the die had been cast. For David Weir, wheelchair racing legend and already proud possessor of three gold medals from London 2012, it was a case of being up early for a close inspection of his kit to see that nothing had been forgotten. Spare tyres, helmet, his racing number, spare gloves, sticky tape for gripping the push rim, a bag of allen keys and every bolt that might be required if the racing chair needed anything corrected at the last minute, all had to be checked off as the Marathon – T54 drew nearer. The air was electric with expectation. Weir had advised the many debutants in the ParalympicsGB team that they should relish and soak up the atmosphere of London 2012. 'There will never be as great a Games in history for British Paralympians,' he claimed. He had waxed lyrical about the facilities in London and admitted to being 'amazed' at his own success. Now, with three gold medals safely tucked away, Weir had one last, huge race ahead of him.

For his coaches, Jenny Archer and Peter Eriksson, they wanted one more big push from him. They knew that, having won the London Marathon six times before and having raced it for over a decade, despite the changed course for the Paralympic Games, focus and muscle memory, allied with the presence he now had over his rivals, could carry Weir home. Canadian racing legend Jeff Adams, an analyst for Channel 4's coverage of the Paralympic Games, reckoned that Weir had finally 'perfected technique and tactics coming into the greatest moment of his career'. This was the time to prove it, over the challenge of a changed and undulating course.

Three track events, three gold medals. 'It feels a bit bizarre saying these have been the easiest races of my career, but I suppose that's what being at the peak of your powers feels like. I don't mean those three finals were easy physically, by any stretch of the imagination. They went perfectly for me in tactical terms, and things just worked out,' the Paralympic champion explained. What Weir could not see from the outside was the deflation on the faces of the defeated. Men who had beaten him before. Yet true to character, he still played his accomplishments down. 'I've overachieved,' he revealed, on the eve of the Marathon – T54. 'I know I've got one more race, but I was aiming for one gold medal and I've got three so far. I've amazed myself at how much speed and endurance I've had. In the final preparation sessions coming into these Games I was getting faster and faster in training and I thought "This is great". I just felt better than I've ever been before and I didn't think that was ever going to happen again. I thought I'd peaked at 27.'

Now the final challenge, the Marathon – T54, lay ahead. There were 63 turns in the course, not a long enough stretch, according to Weir, to create a massive gap. Kurt Fearnley, the reigning Marathon – T54 champion, was in the race and had yet to shine at London 2012. Weir had been watching DVDs of the course on his laptop. Technical, twisty, he was only too well aware that it would be a tough race, and that anything could go wrong. Punctures occur regularly in Marathon racing.

Weir predicted a pack of four or five were likely to be together drafting – taking turns to take the wind with those behind sitting in the slipstream, where you can ease off the work rate – and that the race might well end with a sprint finish down The Mall. He felt energised by the support of the British public. 'You can't describe what it feels like, having capacity crowds even in the morning sessions who are there for you,' he explained. 'I didn't think this would ever happen in Paralympic sport, and it's proven that they're there to watch sport, not disability. That the public are there for you, supporting you, is something that will live with me forever.'

The two years leading up to the London 2012 Games had laid the foundations for Weir's exceptional success. So, from May, had the twelve weeks of driving himself through the pain barrier behind a group of ex-professional cyclists around Richmond Park. They had been there for him, just as the 80,000 fans in the Olympic Stadium and the spectators who lined London's streets were there for the steely-faced athlete every time he pushed his way to glory.

It feels strange to remember that, many years ago, the Paralympic Games had been a black spot in Weir's career. A gold medal eluded him at Atlanta 1996, he missed Sydney 2000 through injury and at Athens 2004, when he expected to win gold, he took a silver medal in the 100m – T54. Such results had left lingering doubts about how good he was, no matter who it was convincing him of the power he had inside him. Internally, he wondered if he had it. Then he turned to Jenny Archer, the coach who had spotted the potential of an eight-year-old boy attending the London Youth Games.

Archer began to build Weir's inner belief after Athens 2004. There was a transformation at Beijing 2008, where he won the 800m – T54 and 1500m – T54, but still doubts persisted. Going into the London 2012 Games, Weir admitted that he would be happy 'with one gold'. Yet Archer, and UK Athletics Paralympic Head Coach Peter Eriksson, had devised a programme for Weir coming into London 2012. They allowed him to miss the warm weather training camp in Portugal. Instead, Weir had stayed at home, racing with his group of high-level cyclists in Richmond Park to fine-tune track and roadwork. The strategy was to lead Weir to 'the most fulfilling race' of his career and a gold medal in the 5000m – T54. This victory set off the gold rush in a way he had only dreamt of.

Something changed in the south Londoner's psyche in November 2010. Minutes after winning the New York Marathon for the first time, he came into a press conference high up in the Mandarin Oriental hotel beside Central Park, beaming from ear to ear. My first thought was that something must be wrong because Weir rarely smiled, especially when he was around the media, or 'at work' in racing mode. He proceeded to explain in detail his delight at the new chair that he had just raced in. It had been created to hug his body like a glove. He admitted that he felt 'a oneness' with his new chair. 'This is the one, mate,' he said. 'They've made perfection. It fits me like a glove, and it's just brilliant.' Weir had never won the Marathon in New York before, and he was made up. 'I'm ready for London now,' he added. 'I've finally arrived.'

Wheelchair racers need to feel the effortless glide in a chair, as if it is a part of them. That moment may well have been the turning point in Weir's career, both in confidence and in dealing with the media. Having known Weir since he was 16, back to the days of his first Paralympic Games, I see the changes in the man and technique are both enormous. After Atlanta 1996 he went home without a medal, a rookie with bags of talent, but bitterly disappointed. He was gruff with the media in those days, almost to the point of being difficult. Smiles were rare. Once you'd got to know him, and earned his trust, he opened up. But he was never a talker, preferring to let his powerful physique, muscular arms and hands of steel speak for him. Looking back, in retrospect, it was a lack of confidence. In fact, even at the London 2012 Paralympic Games, he would ideally have punched the air in salute to 80,000 delirious fans in the Olympic Stadium and fore-gone any media work, happily just heading home.

Mean, moody and magnificent sums the man up. Fortunately, he agrees. On form, he is exactly that. Weir has never moved far from the south London council estate where he was born with a transection of the spine that left him unable to walk. He was raised with his three brothers by his mother Jackie and his father, also David. He was never considered as having a disability. His mother simply worried about him using a wheelchair as it meant he could not travel to schools on buses, as he had done initially, walking with the use of calipers, and of crutches. His father was a soldier in the Irish Guards who has since moved back to Northern Ireland. His parents sat side by side watching his victories in the Olympic Stadium during the Games.

Weir has long been 'Tough of the Track', a no-nonsense person for whom athletic success remains an obses-sion. The bullish neck, the tattooed arms, and the love of House music are simply emblematic of his true nature: a blue-collar man who sits happily in the pub with the same mates he has had since he was a teenager. He has enjoyed stints at DJ-ing, and still mixes tracks.

Weir hates travelling and being away from his family, so that use of home advantage worked to perfection. 'A happy Dave Weir is a winning Dave Weir,' Baroness Grey-Thompson had rightly put it, just a day into the Games. His partner Emily, eight months pregnant with the couple's second child, had come to the Olympic Stadium for his first heat in the 5000m – T54 on the Friday night. It had proved an emotional experience for her. They decided it would be best if she watched the rest of the track events from home, with 12-month-old son Mason.

As Weir had been training for both track races and the Marathon for the first time in his Paralympic career, Archer created a programme whereby the cyclists took him through their gears on both flat and hilly terrain. Weir followed in the slipstream, and took the lead at times in punishing sessions. He reckons that strategic plan brought him into the Games at peak fitness. He was even smuggled out of the Olympic and Paralympic Village and along Olympic lanes to secret training sessions in Richmond Park, near his home, where he had trained for over 15 years. He had his routines. All was familiar. It meant the pressure cooker of a home Games never got going inside his head.

Other circumstances helped, too. Initially, he had been earmarked to compete in ten races, with heats, semi-finals and finals scheduled for the 5000m – T54, 1500m – T54 and 800m – T54. In the week of the Opening Ceremony, the International Paralympic Committee reduced the heats to semi-finals, because the number of competitors was not high enough to include heats. Participating in 'just' seven races instead of an expected ten worked in Weir's favour as the Marathon approached. He had more left in his tank than he might have imagined, or than he could have planned for.

On Day Four of the Games, Weir took the 5000m – T54, the first of four golds that unfolded in a sequence that he described as being like a dream. He'd set a time of 11:27.87 in qualifying for the final, then stormed to victory in a time of 11:07.65 in the Olympic Stadium, thanking the crowd for giving him 'a massive lift'. The sprint finish created a wall of sound in the Stadium.

With the 5000m – T54 under his belt, the strategy was to attack in both 1500m – T54 and 800m – T54 finals. Poise, power and tactical acumen were the key, and they were to take Weir across the line in all three races. The sequence continued on Day Six with his 1500m – T54 title defence, his fourth race of the Games, in a time of 3:12.09. The tabloids were now calling him the 'Weir Wolf', howling their support for him, while some were even wearing masks of the racer's face. He had become a totem to the British spirit of the Games.

Weir was now ultra-confident, taking the lane two position in every heat and final, secure that he could power away in the final 200m. In the 800m – T54 final on Day Eight, he clocked a time of 1:37.63 to claim his third track gold in five days. Weir said after the race that he felt 'on top of the world' and that all three gold medals were 'special'. Weir was now feeding off the energy of the crowd, relishing a national prominence he had never experienced before.'I'm not one for huge emotion, but the roar is unbelievable. Many people have been in touch, including many of the commentators, to say it reminded them off the Mo Farah moment during the Olympic Games. That is some comparison.'

It takes over a decade, Adams reckons, to smooth the

right arm action, strengthen the fingers and wrists and develop the upper-body strength to propel athlete and chair at speeds up to 36 miles an hour on the track. When Weir had sprinted to his third Paralympic gold on the track, Baroness Grey-Thompson, commentating for the BBC high up in the press tribunes, wiped tears from her eyes. The Baroness had singled Weir out at a young age as a future star, and had long been one of his mentors. She had also encouraged and cajoled and advised him, from boy to man.

Weir reserved great credit for his coach. 'Jenny's an amazing woman. She doesn't get the plaudits she deserves. She stays behind the scenes and doesn't do a lot of interviews. I'm so thankful to her for all she has done for me,' he said. He admitted, and it was genuine, that he did not know what he had left in the tank. He had never combined track and Marathon racing at a Paralympic Games. 'I don't know how my body will respond to racing the Marathon on Sunday, as I've never experienced such a sequence,' he explained.

In the 48 hours between winning the third gold and the Marathon – T54, Weir relaxed with his family. He rested mind and body. It was true, he just didn't know what he had left in the tank. There was lots of physiotherapy, sleeping, recovery drinks and long baths, good nutrition, healthy food, early nights. And hours spent with his family. Then on the Sunday morning he rose early, having left the Paralympic Village on the previous afternoon to stay at a hotel around the corner from Buckingham Palace. It meant no travelling on the day of the race.

The Marathon – T54 course was complex, not the the London Marathon one Weir had won a record six times previously. Yet on the final day of the Paralympic Games, the climax to a glorious summer of sport, the champion timed it to perfection. He took a group of racers, including arch-rivals Marcel Hug of Switzerland and Fearnley (AUS), into the final twists of the course before outstripping them on the final bend. In a glorious finale he sprinted down The Mall and over the line to claim gold, winning the Marathon in a time of 1:30:20.

Weir's four gold medals – defending the 800m and 1500m – T54 titles from Beijing 2008, while adding the 5000m and Marathon – T54 crowns – raised the racer to the highest rung in a pantheon of the greatest competitors in Paralympic history. There is a very strong argument to make Weir the greatest wheelchair racer of all time. He joined a hall of fame after the London 2012 Paralympic Games: Swiss racers Heinz Frei, a Paralympic champion on the track and in the Marathon at the same Games; Franz Nietlispach; Canadian Jeff Adams; and the women racers Tanni Grey-Thompson, Chantal Petitclerc of Canada and Louise Sauvage of Australia. Together they comprised the greatest group of all time.

After the race Weir paid tribute to the generous home support all the British athletes received during the Games. 'It didn't matter what position you came in, they were still behind you and they still loved you,' he noted. He had achieved on home ground, in his city, at the last event of a magnificent Parlaympic Games. It was the perfect time to deliver the final stroke of genius on a wonderful summer, etching himself into the history books as one of the brightest stars of London 2012.

The Comeback King Takes his Place in History

Andrew Longmore

Ben Ainslie defies injury and frustration to become the greatest-ever Olympic sailor

On his rest day, the fourth day of the Olympic Sailing regatta at Weymouth and Portland, Ben Ainslie lay on his bed in the team hotel, nursing a sore back and a bruised ego. His hopes of winning a fourth Olympic gold medal – his fifth medal in all – and of becoming the greatest Olympic sailor of all time lay in tatters, and he did not quite know why. He turned on the television to watch the finals of the Rowing at Eton Dorney and saw Helen Glover and Heather Stanning take Britain's first gold of the Games. But Ainslie did not move: he could not. His back was so close to breaking down completely that he had arranged for a helicopter to be on standby, ready to fly him to see a specialist. He just needed the pain to go away, and the only option available was to have an epidural. It had worked before and, though no one recommended painkilling injections as a long-term solution, it could work again. Besides, right then, with his Olympic ambitions slipping away, he needed a quick fix. The long term would look after itself.

He had never suffered a serious injury before, always

presuming himself immune to such nuisances, but he could blame no one but himself for the trouble. Ainslie had pulled the gentlemanly sport of Finn sailing into a new era of professionalism, not just in terms of preparation and tactics, but also physically. Ainslie doesn't just sail a boat, he manhandles it, squeezes every last ounce of speed from it by rocking and pushing and working, like a windsurfer, to catch every wave and every swell. This aggressively physical style of sailing lies at the heart of Ainslie's prolonged domination of the Finn class, in which he had already won two golds. By common consent Ainslie is the best downwind sailor anyone has ever seen. By the start of his fifth Olympic Games at the age of 35, however, he was starting to pay the price for all the hard hours on the water and in the gym, to pay the price of his own excellence. The next generation of sailors, even many of his peers, had begun to copy his technique and it had not helped the strain on his back that, having come straight into his Olympic campaign from helming an America's Cup boat, he needed to increase his weight and power to compete with the rest of the field. His back had been fine through the summer, but a long and bumpy bus ride on a training camp three weeks before the Games had made it worse again.

I had gone down to Falmouth in May to talk to Ainslie before the Finn world championships. He spoke quite candidly of how much his back operation during the winter had scared him. 'There were times when I wasn't sure I would make it back for the Olympic Games,' he'd said. 'I was in a lot of pain, working quite hard at rehab and it wasn't getting any better. I couldn't even stand up without pain and the Olympic Games was just six months away. It felt for me like the whole world was falling down.' He had watched a documentary presented by Andrew Flintoff on how athletes can suffer from depression, and for the first time glimpsed a hidden world. Ainslie had never sought out a sports psychologist in his life and he did not intend to do so now, but injury had made him more aware of his own fragility, in body and in mind. To add to his woes through the winter, the Royal Yachting Association was due to adjudicate on a disrepute charge which stemmed from the world championships in Perth at the end of 2011.

Angered by the repeated incursions on his racing line of a media boat, Ainslie had leapt into the water and boarded the offending RIB to confront the crew. There was some pushing and shoving, but nothing worse before the British sailor realised what he had done and swam back to his boat. Quite rightly, Ainslie was disqualified from the championships, but the RYA had the power to suspend him from further competition, even from the Olympic Games. No one could be quite sure how this august governing body might react to such a blatant breach of sailing's code of conduct. In the end Ainslie was given a slap on the wrist and sent on his way, but the uncertainty and the stress lingered for several months.

Once on the waters of Falmouth Bay, where he had first learned to sail as a child, Ainslie reverted to type, regaining the world title he had lost in Perth and reminding his rivals that the gold in Weymouth was already taken. Maybe, subconsciously, Ainslie went away from Falmouth truly believing in his own invincibility. If so, by the end of race six on the third day of the Olympic regatta, the leader board for the 'men's One Person Dinghy (Heavyweight) Class' provided a very rude awakening. It showed Ainslie trailing Jonas Høgh-Christensen, the Dane, by 10 points, a huge margin. To make matters worse Høgh-Christensen, a talented but notoriously brittle sailor, had shown no signs of cracking under pressure.

On Tuesday I travelled down to Weymouth to see what was happening. Ainslie had endured another frustrating day. He had sailed well, finishing fourth and third, but not well enough to beat the Dane, who had added another first and second to his increasingly impressive list of results. But it was Ainslie's appearance in front of the waiting media that was more shocking. At the end of each day, the sailors have to pass through what is known as the 'mixed zone' to answer questions from press and radio journalists. Iain Percy, who with Andrew Simpson was leading the Star Class, was all business. 'What do you want to know?' he barked at us. When Ainslie came through, he appeared surprisingly calm. There was no sign of the anger or simmering intent that had marked his moods at Athens 2004 and Beijing 2008. He looked beaten, dazed, resigned. He'd lost six races in a row to a Danish sailor he would expect to beat eight times out of ten. Ainslie had been outsailed on his home waters, and he had no real idea how to stem the flow of defeat. No one had ever beaten him six times in a row. In another delicious irony it was a Dane, Paul Elvström, whose record Ainslie was trying to beat to become the greatest Olympic sailor in history.

By the middle of the rest day, Ainslie was starting to feel better. By the time he had been on the physio's table for another prolonged session, he had begun to feel much better. He lay back on his bed again and turned on the television to watch Bradley Wiggins win the Time Trial. Just a few weeks earlier, Wiggins had become the first British cyclist to win the Tour de France. Now here he was sweeping imperiously to Olympic gold. Wiggins reminded him of someone. Ah yes, himself. 'Bradley made it look so easy,' Ainslie told me a week after the Games. 'I thought to myself: "you're at that level, you've got the ability to do this, so stop messing around". I was sailing too conservatively, not pushing the starts enough, trying not to make stupid mistakes rather than going out and making things happen. I wasn't sailing like Ben Ainslie.'

In retrospect, Ainslie felt the pendulum starting to swing back in his favour on Tuesday, when the Finn course was moved further offshore. Here the waves were bigger and the downwind legs, always his strength, longer. Yet the key race in the whole regatta, the defining race in Ainslie's career, perhaps, the one that opened a very closed door just a fraction was race seven, the first after the rest day. Just as Ainslie had spent his day reflecting on his position, so Høgh-Christensen had taken the day to reflect on his. On the one hand he could not have been better placed; on the other, having raced against him for several years, the Dane knew exactly how the Olympic champion would react to adversity. The thought of playing the hare to Ainslie's hound was not a comforting one. The Dane, twice a world champion, had seen how Ainslie could bully his way into the psyche of his closest competitors and he knew that, over the next few days, his stamina and mental strength would be the subject of intense scrutiny. Høgh-Christensen was a talented sailor, for sure; along with Ainslie the most naturally gifted in the fleet, according to Rafa Trujillo Villar, the veteran Spaniard, but he had taken time out to work in the music business for a couple of years which suggested an old-fashioned, almost Corinthian, attitude to his sport. In a pre-Olympic interview he had spoken of how unfit he had become during his time away from racing and how hard it had been to get back to competitive fitness. Høgh-Christiensen was, he thought, a 'dark horse' at these Olympic Games, unlike Beijing 2008 when he had been one of the favourites, under no pressure. But having sailed almost perfectly through the opening three days, instinctively making all the right decisions, the pressure was building and an Olympic gold, Ainslie's gold, was there for the taking. How good would it be to take a gold medal back to his father, Jorg, who had sailed in the same class at the 1980 Olympic Games?

Race seven realised Høgh-Christensen's worst fears. Ainslie returned to sailing like Ainslie and Jonas returned to sailing like Jonas. It was not just that the Englishman won his first race of the regatta or that he had beaten the Dane for the first time in seven races; it was that he forced Høgh-Christensen into making a crucial mistake. Already beaten, the Dane capsized and finished eighth. Had he stayed upright and cut his losses, he might well have been the champion. In the second race of the day Ainslie prevailed again, narrowly, but encouragingly for the growing band of spectators who had turned The Nothe above the bay into a sea of Union flags. But Høgh-Christensen had made another big mistake. He and the Dutch sailor Pieter-Jan Postma had claimed Ainslie had touched a buoy on the way round the course. Aware of the claim, Ainslie had to make an immediate decision: did he ignore the shouts and try to establish his innocence in the protest room, risking disqualification, or did he take a penalty turn and risk losing the race? He took the penalty turn and still finished third. But he didn't like the protest one bit, and told Høgh-Christensen so in no uncertain terms as the pair crossed the line. He was still seething about the indignity of it all when he came into the mixed zone. 'That's made me angry,' he said. And everyone knew what that meant. Like John McEnroe, Ainslie is one of the few athletes who performs better when he is angry.

Going into the final day before the medal race, Ainslie was still behind, but the gap was closing. In race nine, it was neck and neck, Ainslie sixth, one place behind Høgh-Christensen. In race 10, Ainslie sailed one of the best races of his life to take the victory. But it was not enough. Behind him, Postma and Høgh-Christensen were duelling for second place. If the latter finished third, Ainslie would only have to finish one place ahead of him in the medal race, in which points count double, to secure the gold. So, on the last leg of the race, he dropped back to try and hamper the Dane. It's a legal tactic, if not exactly in the sportsman's handbook. Yet the plan worked perfectly. With Ainslie taking his wind on one side and the Dutchman pushing hard on the other, Høgh-Christensen dropped to third place, and Ainslie still sailed away to win. For the first time in the whole regatta, the equation was balanced on his side. 'It was starting to become fun again,' said Ainslie later. As Sydney, Athens and Beijing had proved, Britain's greatest sailor is never happier than when turning a fleet race into hand-to-hand combat. At the start of the medal race, for the first time in the regatta, Høgh-Christensen began to sail defensively. Instead of racing his own race, he was looking to defend, and Ainslie knew that the intangible force known as momentum had swung his way. He was the attacker now and his prey would not escape.

All the way round the course, Ainslie kept Høgh-Christensen at bay, cutting off his wind supply and covering any tactical moves. It didn't matter that the pair were ninth and tenth, in the last two points-scoring places; Ainslie would still be assured of the gold. Or so he thought. Slowly but surely easing his way through the field was Pieter-Jan Postma. By the last mark the Dutchman had sailed into second place. If Postma won and Ainslie came home ninth, Postma would take the Olympic title. Barely had the commentators and spectators realised the danger than Postma made a fatal error. In trying to sneak through an impossible gap to take the lead, Postma touched the boat of New Zealander Dan Slater, incurring an automatic two-turn penalty. Postma dropped out of the medal standings and Ainslie's place in history was assured.

His first reaction to his fourth Olympic gold was relief, his second was shock. When a BBC reporter stuck a microphone under his nose and enthused about his being the greatest Olympic sailor of all time, Ainslie could think of nothing meaningful to say. So he just said 'Yeah'. He lit two red flares and held them aloft in a pose reminiscent of round-the-world sailors returning to port. But Ainslie does not much like the limelight. He is a shy man, at his happiest out on the water perfecting his craft and winning races. On the way back into the harbour, the camera caught him giving his boat a few pats on the side, like a jockey down a horse's neck. A week later he would sail his beloved *Rita*, the boat that had carried him to three Olympic gold medals, up the Thames past the Houses of Parliament, before gifting her to the National Maritime Museum in Falmouth. That night he was wined and dined in the Painted Hall at the Royal Naval College in Greenwich and garlanded with praise by sponsors and guests. Delightfully, Ainslie looked thoroughly embarrassed by all the attention. He may never race a Finn dinghy again, but has not ruled out returning to a less physically demanding Olympic class in the future. In the meantime, he has an America's Cup to win for Britain, the first since 1851. After one of the most extraordinary comebacks in Olympic Sailing history, nothing is beyond the reach of the sport's greatest Olympian.

Natural Born Talent

Gareth A Davies

Sarah Storey's fourth gold of London 2012 makes her the most decorated British competitor of the modern Paralympic Games

The final gold medal, for the Road Race – C4/5, capped a momentous week for Sarah Storey. It joined her growing pile of London 2012 golds: her first in Road Cycling, the Time Trial – C5, plus a brace in Track events: the Pursuit – C5 and the 500m Time Trial – C4/5. On the home straight in that final race, the Road Race – C4/5, an incredible seven minutes ahead of her rivals, the 34-year-old had relaxed and showboated, raising her left hand to salute the cheering throng while freewheeling to the line. She even admitted feeling slightly guilty about it afterwards, typical of the arch-critic and perfectionist that she is. As his wife crossed the line at Brands Hatch to record her fourth gold medal, her husband Barney Storey, himself competing in the Paralympic Games, roared 'You're a legend!'

She had ridden herself into the record books by claiming a total of 11 gold medals, first in Swimming, then in Cycling, from six consecutive Paralympic Games. Praise was heaped on her after her victory, with Shane Sutton, head coach of Team GB Cycling, reckoning Sarah was akin to 'Usain Bolt or Sir Chris Hoy in the Paralympic

Games'. The event had become an incredible 'Storey' for the cyclist and her husband, formerly a professional cyclist and now a non-disabled pilot in the Sprint – B, for partially sighted riders. Storey, the outstanding British female Paralympian of London 2012, was feted after her dominant display over the field at Brands Hatch. She even overtook some of the competitors in the men's race, which had started earlier.

She had achieved so much at London 2012. On the first day of competition in the Velodrome, she swept to victory in the Individual Pursuit – C5 final, to claim the opening gold of London 2012 for a jubilant ParalympicsGB. It was the eighth of Storey's own career. She had also broken a world record in the qualifying round – for the 72nd time in her seven-year cycling career. As the medals mounted up, the champion found time to reflect, and to relish. On securing her second gold she made the journey from the Paralympic Village to the news conference in ParalympicsGB House, beside Westfield Shopping Centre – only 200m – on her winning bicycle. Call it superstition, but she was not letting it out of her sight.

The quadruple gold triumph put her on the front page of most national newspapers. 'Stirring Storey', 'Same old Storey', 'Storey of true grit', and the inevitable 'Fairy Storey' … the press may have been running out of superlatives to describe her performances, yet the puns were never-ending. Privately the level-headed lass from Manchester was probably chuckling. Her life had been planned around winning, and competing from a young age.

In the warm glow of a successful home Games, she looked back over the last 20 years. There were so many people to thank in what she acknowledges was a collective effort of teachers, coaches, parents and husband.

Blessed with a natural athletic prowess, she had never allowed her disability to hinder her progress as a child – in sport or in life outside it. Young Sarah Bailey's dreams were first set in place watching Sarah Hardcastle, Daley Thompson and Tessa Sanderson at the Los Angeles 1984 Games. She caught one-handed, and learned how to address her balance when running. The champion athlete praised the teachers who had first nurtured her love of sport at Disley Primary School. These, she admitted, had been important and formative years for her sporting career that lay ahead. Fittingly, one of the gold post-boxes that the Royal Mail has painted in her honour is at Poynton, just down the road from her former school. In Storey's day there had been a sporting centre for excellence at Disley – not anything formal, but unusual: the school's swimming club was run by parents on a Saturday afternoon. Headteacher Chris Parker had believed in sport as development, convinced that it made the children more productive in the classroom.

Young Sarah Bailey did gymnastics and played for the boys' cricket team. She was also a member of the table tennis team that was enrolled in an adult league, and Mr Parker used to drive the team to matches. 'Tough times never last, but tough people do,' he told Storey, and she has never forgotten the aphorism. She ran cross country for the school for five years, and also for the county of Cheshire, as well as competing in the national schools cross country championships, finishing in the top 20 in the country for her age group. Through it all she had great parental support and great coaches. Her father built an extension at her home so that she could have a games room in which to practise. Throughout her teenage years, a Saturday would involve an early morning at Stockport for swimming, competing in a cross country race during the day and then, the mud washed away, a dash in the car to a table tennis tournament in the afternoon.

At Poynton High School, there was no letting up in Storey's sporting prowess. She captained the school and county netball teams up to under-16 level and then, in 1992, the shy 14-year-old attended her first Paralympic Games in Barcelona. Having been fast-tracked into the squad, she ended up taking six Swimming medals: two golds, three silvers and a bronze. Yet when the county netball team found out that she had competed at the Barcelona Paralympic Games and taken gold medals there, they dropped her from the squad.

Storey believes that sport and academia go hand in hand – a philosophy on which the Government might well ask her to advise. She used to recite French and German verbs and construct essays in her head when she was running or swimming in training. She had even contemplated becoming a Physical Education teacher, and does still spend the odd day teaching sport at schools in Salford. 'Perhaps I'm lucky that I've got an almost photographic memory and quite an efficient mind, but I did get bullied slightly in school because I was so immersed in my sport. I even did an 'A' Level on the morning of the Opening Ceremony of the Atlanta 1996 Paralympic Games,' she told me some time ago.

Storey has never been hampered in her pursuit of sporting excellence because she was born without a left hand, or because she has suffered from both asthma and chronic fatigue. They have just been obstacles for her to leap over and surpass, in her race to become one of Britain's greatest multi-sport athletes. At times she has had to battle prejudice, like many Paralympians. When she returned from Atlanta in 1996, to start life as an undergraduate at Leeds University, for instance, her attempt to join the city's swimming club was not successful. The head coach simply told her that they did not work with disabled swimmers. She joined Stockport Swimming Club instead and never looked back, winning more medals at both Sydney 2000 and Athens 2004. Yet the travelling eventually took its toll, and she suffered with chronic fatigue.

Remarkably, she only discovered her talent at cycling after a chronic ear infection in 2004 kept her out of the water for six months. She took up cycling to stay fit and, in her own words, she got so 'carried away' that she switched careers the following year. Given her perseverance, dedication and ability to push herself, you suspect that Storey would have achieved elite status in whichever sphere she decided to apply herself. She is just one of those people who have it all. And then some.

At the Manchester Velodrome Storey found a second calling as a sportswoman. It was also there that she met her future husband Barney. Love and athleticism blossomed together, with Sarah Bailey, once renowned as a swimmer, becoming Sarah Storey, ambitious cyclist, in 2007. They have become an incredible team, as coach and rider, husband and wife, with a deep knowledge and understanding of one another. 'She likes challenges herself. It's about pushing back boundaries with her,' says Barney, an insulin-dependent diabetic since the age of four. Attention to detail was key, and Barney admits that even he is amazed at her perspicacity. 'Sarah is a complete perfectionist; she works everything out for herself, and is so competitive. Even when we have ridden a tandem together she wants to steer it from behind.'

Sarah, for her part, reserves high praise for her adviser

husband. 'Barney is my mechanic. He has helped me to re-form my body position in the saddle, so it is more aerodynamic, and I'm going to keep pushing myself. His expertise in cycling is just phenomenal,' she explains. 'Before he was a tandem pilot he was a non-disabled solo cycling sprinter, riding World Cup events. Barney has an immense knowledge of cycling. I came along, this raw swimmer with big shoulders and he moulded me into the cyclist I am today.' For the couple, London 2012's streets truly turned to gold. While Sarah dominated her C5 classification group to claim four gold medals, Barney took a gold and silver in the Velodrome as pilot to Neil Fachie, the visually impaired Scotsman.

Minutes after Storey's victory at Brands Hatch, wheelchair racing legend Baroness Grey-Thompson called to congratulate her on drawing level with her own gold medal tally, and that of swimmer David Roberts. 'Tanni is a good friend of mine and an amazing lady,' observed the champion. 'She was my mentor at Barcelona in 1992 when I was young Sarah Bailey, just 14, and to equal her record is amazing, absolutely immense. I'll keep striving to win medals as long as I am fit enough, and the selectors keep picking me. It's what you can do, not what you can't, that makes you a Paralympian and a winner.'

She had become only the sixth British Paralympian – after swimmers Roberts, Chris Holmes and Mike Kenny, Tanni Grey-Thompson and cyclist Darren Kenny – to win four or more gold medals in a single Paralympic Games. Storey, Grey-Thompson and Roberts all have eleven Paralympic gold medals. Overall Sarah has now been awarded 22 medals at six Games, making her the most decorated British competitor of the modern Paralympic Games.

Remarkably, Storey is still improving, with Cycling at

the Olympic Games still within her reach. She had been in contention for Team GB's Olympic Team Pursuit squad for London 2012, riding non-disabled World Cup events before being cut from the eventual line-up. Competing against non-disabled rivals, she was sixth in the 3000m individual pursuit at the 2010 Commonwealth Games, representing England.

There was no issue with the selection from Storey, only disappointment. The team eventually selected, Laura Trott, Dani King and Jo Rowsell, powered to gold in a succession of world record times. Her ambitions still burn brightly, however. With the international cycling federation apparently ready to give women parity with the men by introducing a four-rider, 4000m Team Pursuit, Storey could conceivably ride at Rio 2016 in both the Olympic and Paralympic Games. And for the legendary Paralympian, reaching the Rio 2016 Olympic Games with the women's Team Pursuit squad or whichever other event she throws herself into, is next on the agenda.

After winning her fourth gold medal at London 2012, she pledged to keep going until Rio in four years time. Few competitors in history have done 'the double' and competed at both Games, including: 'Blade Runner' Oscar Pistorius as a 400m runner, for South Africa; Natalia Partyka, a Table Tennis player who has no arm just below her elbow, for Poland; Natalie du Toit, an open water and pool swimmer, who retired after the London 2012 Games; and Pal Szekeres. He first competed as an non-disabled fencer at the Seoul 1988 Olympic Games, where he won bronze in the Team Foil event. In 1991 he was injured in a bus accident, and went on to compete as a wheelchair fencer a year later at Barcelona 1992, taking a gold medal. Szekeres also competed at London

2012, his sixth Paralympic Games.

One issue which Storey feels she has highlighted is the talent pool within the UK that goes untapped. She is aware that many people with the physiology to be an athlete may have never realised it, or had the opportunity or confidence to develop sporting skills. Changing the arbitariness of access to sport is, she hopes, part of the legacy of London 2012, as spectators inspired by the events they have seen are encouraged to try them out. Only then can they start to realise their talents. 'How many gold medallists – Olympic and Paralympic – have we got out there who don't even realise it?' she speculates.

Storey's philosophy, as might be expected from one so determined to push to the limit, is never to accept limitations. 'Don't ever put any limits on yourself,' she urges. 'People and external influences may try to persuade you to go in other directions, but I believe there are no such things as boundaries. You can give anything a go – it doesn't even matter if you don't succeed in it. If you had told me 20 years ago, when I was just starting my GCSEs, that I would be going to Games number six as a cyclist, and would have six Cycling gold medals to my name, and ambitions to compete in the Olympics, too, then I would have laughed at you. If you have an open mind, anything is possible.'

For those who watched Storey in the Velodrome and at Brands Hatch, riding with composure and conviction into Paralympic history, her victories represent more than another Cycling medal. They are the affirmation of a belief in one's potential, a determination to achieve the incredible. Inspiring and encouraging in so many areas, you know that for her, at least, life really is that way.

The Golden Mobot

Simon Turnbull

Mo Farah joins long-distance greats with dramatic Olympic double

It's 7.43pm on Saturday 11 August 2012 in London, and the Olympic Stadium is a crucible of noise. The 80,000-strong crowd has been whipped up to fever pitch, watching the last laps of the men's 5000m final. A stick-insect figure of a Londoner leads into the home straight, but it seems like he has the world gathering at his shoulder, ready to pounce.

In fact, there have been five men chasing hard on the heels of Mo Farah since the clanging sound of the bell. Two of them are threatening to overtake: Thomas Longosiwa of Kenya and Dejen Gebremeskel of Ethiopia. The finish line is less than 100m ahead. Immortality beckons.

Only six of the all-time greats of distance running have managed to complete the coveted 5000m–10,000m double in the 112-year history of the modern Olympic Games. Hannes Kolehmainen, the original Flying Finn, was the first to achieve the feat, at Stockholm 1912, precisely a century ago. Then came Emil Zátopek, the Czech soldier, at Helsinki 1952, followed by Vladimir Kuts of the Soviet Union at Melbourne four years later.

Lasse Virén, the Finnish policeman, even did it twice over, at Munich 1972 and at Montreal four years later.

Then there was Miruts Yifter – 'Yifter the Shifter', as the BBC television commentator David Coleman memorably christened him. The balding Ethiopian took gold in both distances at the Moscow 1980 Games. Then, four years ago at Beijing, there was another Ethiopian, the phenomenal Kenenisa Bekele, at the peak of his powers.

Having won the 10,000m in style seven days previously – clinching a third British gold in the space of 45 minutes on 'Super Saturday' – Farah now stood on the threshold of an achievement that, in the opinion of no less an authority than Lord Coe, would elevate him to the status of 'greatest British track and field Olympian of all time'.

The mind freeze-frames the picture of the Somali-born Briton hanging on to pole position and spools back to a Saturday afternoon in January. Farah is sitting in the restaurant at Lornah Kiplagat's High Altitude Training Centre in Iten, Kenya. The 'University of Champions', it says on the sign outside. He has been here for two months – away from his wife, Tania, and daughter, Rihanna – putting in the hard yards, or rather the 120 miles a week, on the red dust trails that wind around the tiny Kenyan hill town that stands 7,800ft above sea level, overlooking the vast, breathtaking sweep of the Great Rift Valley. Farah has been so immersed in laying the foundation for the home Olympic Games that he has no idea of the actual dates when the 5000m and 10,000m will take place in London. 'Paula Radcliffe had to tell me', he confesses.

'I like it here,' Farah continues. 'The life is easy. You sleep. You train. There are no distractions.' That is not quite true. The local track in this global distance running Mecca is not exactly of Olympic standard. Cattle have been known to wander on to it. Farah laughs. 'There was a classic one yesterday,' he says. 'There were donkeys on the track. I shouted to try to scare them off. They were in lane one so I had to go on a different bit of the track. I've got a picture of them on my camera.'

Back in the here and now of Saturday 11 August, thousands of cameras are flashing around the Olympic Stadium. They are capturing the vital moments of Mo Farah's date with destiny, the date Paula Radcliffe so kindly identified for him. Thankfully, there are no donkeys on the inside lane. Ahead of the thoroughbred Farah is a clear run to the winner's enclosure. As the line approaches, first Longosiwa and then Gebremeskel attempt to get past. Roared on by deafening cheers, the Mighty Mo resists. He surges forward to victory and into the annals of history, crossing the line 0.32 ahead of Gebremeskel, with Longosiwa in the bronze medal position. The winning time, a pedestrian 13:41.66, is an irrelevance. The achievement is anything but.

Farah wears a wide-eyed expression of disbelief. He stretches his arms out in triumph, then puts his hands to his head in an 'M' shape. All around the arena, the crowd and purple-shirted volunteers are performing 'the Mobot'. The trademark celebration was born when Farah appeared on the TV show A League Of Their Own and presenter James Corden suggested he should create a victory pose to match that of Usain Bolt. Guest Clare Balding suggested outlining an 'M' shape above his head, as in the style of the Village People's YMCA. Corden christened it the Mobot.

The race won, the double completed, Farah drops to his knees on the track and performs some sit-ups. The familiar sound of David Bowie comes blasting over the public address system. A hero just for one day? For the rest of his life, more like. After two Super Saturdays, Mo

Farah's life has changed forever. Chants of 'Mo! Mo! Mo!' ring around the arena. In the last track final of the night Usain Bolt crosses the finish line – performing the Mobot as he anchors home the Jamaican 4 x 100m Relay team in world record time. He later joins Farah on the podium, trading poses. 'I can't believe he did the Mobot as he was breaking a world record,' Farah reflects. 'Me and Usain get on really well. We go back a long way. We've had the same agent for years – Ricky Simms.'

Farah has some way to go yet to get on level terms with the Lightning Bolt as a global phenomenon, but with his home Olympic heroics he has elevated himself to the status of national treasure – and also to that of all-time great. For all of Britain's rich history as a distance running nation, no previous stars had managed to win a single Olympic title at the 5000m or 10,000m. Brendan Foster had high hopes of the double at Montreal 1976. He finished third in the 10,000m, then fifth in the 5000m. 'Yes, some of us tried,' the BBC television commentator says. 'Some of us came close. And now Mo has done it. Fantastic. I am loving saying, "Mo Farah, double Olympic champion". He's such a lovely lad, too. It couldn't have happened to a nicer person.'

Anyone who has encountered the 29-year-old ray of sunshine on his path to Olympic greatness would agree.

Mohammad Farah was born in Mogadishu, Somalia, on 23 March 1983. He spent much of his early life living in Djibouti and moved to England at the age of eight to settle with his father in west London. On his first day at junior school he was teased for his lack of English, picked a fight with the toughest kid in the playground, and was given a black eye for his trouble. It was his PE teacher at Feltham Community College, Alan Watkinson, who got the football-loving, Arsenal-besotted Farah into running. 'He had the bare minimum,' Watkinson recalls. 'He had his trainers and his school uniform. He couldn't afford spikes or any specialist athletics equipment. People pulled around and supported him.'

It was the same when Farah first made it on to the international scene. A week before his 17th birthday, in March 2000, he ran in the junior race at the World Cross Country Championships in Vilamoura, Portugal. He finished 25th. 'I can remember Mo with his dreadlocks, running around the pool and getting told off, saying "Can't you stop that noisy little boy jumping in the pool?"' Paula Radcliffe recalls. The noisy little boy was a party animal and something of a smiling teenage tearaway, renowned for stripping naked and jumping into the Thames off Kingston Bridge. Still, Radcliffe saw the potential world-beater in the teenage Mo. She paid for him to have driving lessons so that he could get to training sessions more easily.

Others also saw the potential and patiently nurtured it. They included Simms, a former Irish under-23 runner, who took the young Farah on to the books of the Teddington-based PACE Sports Management, Alan Storey, the distance running coach who guided Mike Leod, Britain's last Olympic 10,000m medallist, and McLeod, the Tynesider who took silver in the 25-lap event at the Los Angeles 1984 Games.

A pivotal part of Farah's development was moving in with some of Simms' Kenyan athletes and learning to follow their simple, near-monastic lifestyle of eat, sleep and train. The rewards came at the 2010 European Athletics Championships in Barcelona. Farah was untouchable in the 5000m and 10,000m. He was the king of continental distance running – but it was the global crown that he wanted.

Thus, in February 2011, he packed his bags and headed

to Oregon with Tania and Rihanna in tow. In a bid to acquire the cutting edge to take on the world's best, Farah – who had failed to reach the 5000m final at the Beijing 2008 Games and had finished seventh in the 5000m final at the World Championships in Athletics in Berlin in 2009 – joined the elite group of distance runners coached at Beaverton, on the outskirts of Portland, by Alberto Salazar.

Salazar, a three-time winner of the New York City Marathon, set up his 'Oregon Project' in 2001 in the north-west corner of the United States with the intention of putting USA distance runners back on the podium at global championships. His ultra-holistic approach allies the grind of 120 miles a week in training with the appliance of science.

Salazar's charges use under-water treadmills, anti-gravity treadmills and Cryosauna chambers that blast liquid nitrogen to speed muscle recovery after hard training. 'The Cryosauna was referred to me by the number one NFL trainer in the country, a guy called Tom Shaw,' Salazar says. 'He said his athletes recovered so much quicker with it, so we checked it out. That's my philosophy. We are going to train as hard as anybody else, and then we are going to train more by adding things that don't get us injured. We are going to train smarter than anybody else. It's like in war. The soldier has to learn how to fight and do everything – be physically fit, be a one-man army. But you also try to equip him with every bit of top science – everything you can – to keep him alive. That's what we do. We use science every bit that we can, on top of old-school training.'

The benefits of Salazar's regime were to become apparent at the World Championships in Athletics in Daegu, Korea, in August 2011. Farah took the silver medal in the 10,000m after he was caught napping off the final bend by the unheralded Ibrahim Jeilan of Ethiopia, but was too strong for his rivals when it came to the 5000m.

It was the same in the 10,000m final at London 2012. Farah was content to bide his time back in the pack until hitting the front just before the bell and cranking up the pressure by degrees, like one of the Inquisition's finest thumbscrew operators. It did the trick. As Farah pulled clear to victory in 27:30.42, his joy was compounded when he crossed the line and turned to see his American training partner, Galen Rupp, claiming the silver medal, with Tariku Bekele of Ethiopia third. 'I'm just so happy that Galen finished second,' Farah said. 'We work so hard together and we have a good laugh together. He's one of my best friends.'

Up in the stands, Salazar was close to tears. 'The emotion when they stepped over the line was overwhelming, greater than anything I did in my own athletics career,' he said. 'Apart from getting married and my kids' births, it was the best feeling I've ever had.'

There was to be another winning feeling for coach and athlete a week later. Farah was again happy to play a waiting game when it came to the 5000m final, starting at the very back of the 15-man field as his rivals set off at a dawdle. After 1,000m, he moved from the back to the front, but without injecting any meaningful pace. It was all part of the phoney war. Only with four laps to go did the real battle commence.

Gebremeskel and his Ethiopian teammate Yenew Alamirew were prominent as the pace upped significantly with a 59-second lap. Throughout, as the race built up to a crescendo, Farah maintained the perfect position. With 500m to go, he and Rupp led the way. At the bell Longosiwa tried to force his way past, but Farah held his ground. He continued to do so all the way to the line

– even when the Kenyan and Gebremeskel applied severe pressure. He covered the final mile in 4 minutes exactly and the final lap in a scorching 52.94.

'These two medals are for the girls that Tania is carrying,' Farah reflects, sitting with his golds around his neck in Team GB House. 'They're twins. So there's one each.'

And to think: they might have been two golds by a Flying Dutchman rather than a British Fly Mo. When Farah first headed to Europe as an eight-year-old, he almost went to live with his grandmother in the Netherlands instead of joining his father in London.

As the enormity of his achievement sinks in, he can only reflect on the wisdom of his decision to go west at the start of 2011. 'There were a lot of questions asked at the time because I was double European champion,' Farah says. 'People were saying, "Why are you changing when things are going so well?" But in my mind I knew something had to change. It was a gamble, but if I hadn't made that change I don't think I would be sitting here with two gold medals today. All those guys were queuing up to pass me and I could feel that I wasn't going to let anyone past. It was an incredible feeling. In training I am learning and doing a lot of hard training and I can feel that I am stronger. I wasn't able to finish races strong in the past – I was weak. I knew I had to work on my strength. Alberto said I ran like a girl, in terms of not using my arms when I was sprinting – when I was tired I was all over the place. That's what I mean by weak. So we strengthened my core. Alberto is a genius. He's an honest guy and a great coach.'

Mo Farah is an honest, endearingly grounded guy who happens also to be a truly great athlete. His genial personality lit up London 2012 – and so, unforgettably, did his golden talent. Twice over.

'Let's Dance'

Gareth A Davies

The shining talents of Sophie Christiansen and Rio claim a magnificent third gold to seal record Equestrian success

She had friends and family in the Greenwich Park arena on 3 September 2012, many of whom were watching her compete for the first time in her third Games. Yet Sophie Christiansen showed no sign of nerves, delivering another impeccable performance on her gelding Janeiro, known at home as Rio. Her compelling Freestyle Test: Individual – Grade 1a routine delighted the crowd and earned the 24-year-old a score of 84.750, an extraordinarily consistent achievement at the Paralympic Games. Only six scores above 80 per cent were recorded throughout the week at Greenwich Park – and Christiansen recorded three of those to take her triple gold.

The announcer had asked for silence during the Freestyle Test performance. It was the first time many of the spectators had experienced 'butterfly waving', a feature unique to the sport. Members of the audience are asked not to clap until horse and groom are reunited after the test, particularly in the Freestyle Test: Individual – Grade 1a, and to show their appreciation instead by waving, either hands or flags. The silence this creates is incredibly powerful and moving; Team Manager David Hunter described it as 'so special and poignant'. The atmosphere was not lost on Christiansen, a very special athlete and skilled performer. When, at the denouement of her routine, a supporter screamed out 'Sophie we love you', the arena was suddenly bathed in a wall of applause. She reckoned it was either her cousin or her younger brother Alex, a Games Maker at the event, who uttered the cry. A spell was ended. Horse and rider had 'danced' in perfect symmetry, joyously in tune with the crowd's mood. Janeiro 6 had done his rider proud. 'My horse has a good character, he really likes people,' Sophie explained. 'He just loves being the centre of attention. It all just clicks.'

The year leading up to London 2012 had not been without concerns. In 2011 Christiansen's former horse Rivaldo went lame – the day before she was due to go to the European Championships. Yet on Janeiro 6 she shone, her triple gold at the Paralympic Games establishing her as one of the greatest riders of an exceptional team.

Years of toil and effort have gone into her riding, yet Christiansen made it look easy at London 2012. 'The Games have changed a lot, and we are now pretty professional,' she explained to me. 'The Paralympic Games have really grown so much in the last few years and to have it in London enabled us to show the whole world how Paralympians should be featured.'

Just prior to the Games, she had bubbled with pride at the music tracks she had devised, together with composer Owen Gurry, also a session guitarist. It was designed to reflect her exuberant personality, and would be her crowning moment of the Games. 'My freestyle music for London came about after I made friends with Owen. We constructed a mash-up of orchestral versions of Queen and Pink Floyd and Muse, and then we'd added a bit of

The Beatles,' she revealed. In her own words, she wanted to 'change the face of Dressage music', and to highlight her pride in London and its musical creativity.

Christiansen's repertoire was certainly very different. She began with *I Want It All*, the original work of Queen, then moved into *Another Brick In The Wall* and *I Belong To You* by Muse. Then, as the Big Ben bells tolled, an actor recited John of Gaunt's 'This Sceptred Isle' speech from *Richard II*. The result was stunning. She dominated her Freestyle event with majesty and relish, setting the 11,000-strong crowd alight. She won by a margin of five points to add to the gold medals she won in the Championship Test and Team – Open event.

As far as sports performance goes, the big picture was impressive. Great Britain's Paralympic Equestrian team reached a medal tally of 11: five gold, five silver and one bronze medal. The team thus surpassed its total medal tally record of 10, set at the Beijing 2008 Paralympic Games. On Day Four of the Paralympic Games Britain retained its record of winning a medal in every grade at every Paralympic, World and European championships since the sport became part of the Games at Atlanta 1996. It was the same day that all the British riders competing won an individual medal. Christiansen took Freestyle Test: Individual – Grade 1a gold, Sophie Wells Freestyle Test: Individual – Grade IV silver and Deb Criddle Individual – Grade III silver. The team had delivered an amazing result.

'At Beijing 2008, we won 10 medals with seven riders. Here we've won 11 medals with five riders and exceeded our target,' explained Will Connell, Performance Director for equestrian at UK Sport. 'This is the first time anyone has won medals in all five grades in the Individual and Freestyle.' Team Manager David Hunter echoed his praise of the group's cooperation. 'The atmosphere here has been a huge bonus ... The spectators have been so caring, some knowledgeable, some not, but so enthused. It is the biggest audience, 11,000, that any Para-Equestrian competitor of any nation has ever ridden in front of.'

Christiansen admitted that the quintet – long-established champion Lee Pearson, newcomers Sophie Wells and Natasha Baker, herself and Athens 2004 double gold medallist Deborah Criddle – had all been inspired by their Olympic counterparts who took five medals, including three golds. 'The able-bodied team did brilliantly at the Olympic Games and we were able to feed off that,' she noted. 'There was no pressure – we went to Greenwich feeling inspired by them.'

Christiansen herself is an inspiring young woman: funny, quirky, brainy, brilliant and beautiful. She was born two months prematurely with cerebral palsy so suffered from health issues including jaundice, blood poisoning, a heart attack and a collapsed lung. 'I was born like this. Apparently my umbilical cord got wrapped around my neck and kind of twisted so there was oxygen starvation of my brain, but I think I was just eager to get out. I was fighting from the start. I was eager,' she explained. She took up horse riding at her local Riding for the Disabled Association group aged six as a form of physiotherapy.

Originally from Ascot in Berkshire, Christiansen was educated at Charters School, a comprehensive in Sunningdale which, ahead of its time, had accepted pupils with physical impairments since 1983. Her parents, both teachers, fought for her to go to the mainstream school with a special unit attached, and, in common with many of Britain's Paralympians today, she believes they were right. Christiansen wasn't bullied, nor did she suffer name-calling at school. She was desperately shy, mainly because of her speech, which is slurred but clear, yet by the time she took her GCSEs she had a network of friends. It was also then she started to become prominent as an international rider.

London 2012 was her third Paralympic Games representing Great Britain. She had been the youngest athlete on the team at Athens 2004 where she contested both the Freestyle and Championship – Grade Ia events, the classification grade for athletes with impairments that have the greatest impact on their ability to ride. On her horse, Hotstuff, she took a bronze medal in the latter.

Four years later Christiansen represented Great Britain at the Beijing 2008 Paralympic Games. This time she won three medals, two gold and one silver. The Equestrian events were not held in the Host City of Beijing, but instead took place at the Olympic Equestrian Centre in Hong Kong. The riders, apart from Lee Pearson's exceptional three gold medals (taken for the third time in three consecutive Paralympic Games), went largely under the radar. Competing in her second Games, Sophie again contested the Freestyle and Championship events. She won gold and silver on her horse Lambrusco, taking her second gold as part of the British quartet in the Team – Open. With the team – Christiansen, Pearson, Anne Dunham and Simon Laurens – taking gold, Great Britain had won a gold medal in this event at four consecutive Paralympic Games. London 2012 was no different.

After leaving Sunningdale in 2006 (the year it was marked as 'outstanding' by educational inspectors) Christiansen went on to study for a Masters degree in Mathematics at Royal Holloway, University of London. Over the course of the London Games, thousands of supporters not only discovered her skills, competitiveness and control as a Dressage rider; they also learned of her brilliance at maths and music. A remarkable all-round talent, she had been a model pupil, just as she is a horsewoman. Her success at London 2012 was no flash in the pan.

Christiansen has been changing people's perceptions all her life. As a result of cerebral palsy her limbs are floppy, she has muscle spasms and her head and jaw move sometimes to an accentuated rhythm. 'Because of my speech people think I'm not all there,' she notes wryly. 'When they think I'm mentally disabled, I try to drop in the conversation that I got a first-class Masters degree in maths.' Today, it is not a shy young woman who sets people right. Down the years, having covered five Summer Paralympic Games, I know that Paralympians have a powerful radar in detecting whether people are being genuine or patronising them. Christiansen has this in abundance.

She has always impressed those she meets. After competing at the Athens 2004 Games, aged 16, Sophie inspired Sir Paul McCartney to come to the aid of the team. He launched a £2 million fundraising campaign for ParalympicsGB with London agency Saatchi, showcasing Britain's most successful disabled athletes. Sophie found Sir Paul 'awesome', 'just a normal guy – so down to earth – you forget he is a mega-star'.

That summer, prior to the Beijing 2008 Games, Channel 4 aired the feature, which included various sports and spotlighted the young rider. Subsequent adverts featured Sir Paul, requesting that the public make donations to the team, and he also allowed the iconic *Live and Let Die* soundtrack to be used in the first advertisement. 'When I met Sophie, I was completely blown away by her skill, dedication and the fact that she had won a gold medal for Britain, so I felt I had to do something,' he remarked. 'It was the start of a truly amazing effort from all those involved, most of whom gave their time for free.'

Christiansen is exceptional in many ways. She is a very bright woman, with a strong and captivating personality and a great sense of humour. To meet her is to be changed. One of her aims has always been to get people to understand her disability. 'After Beijing 2008, I had a real think about what I wanted to do because I'd won a Paralympic gold medal. That was always my dream. But I thought "what can I do with this?" I can educate other people in sport and disability. I talk a lot in schools so they can learn both about the Paralympic Games and disability because I think it's the only way people can be exposed to it. There is still a long way to go, but I think we're getting there.' She believes that disabled people have been empowered following the Paralympic Games. There is still much work to be done, however, not least in improving transport facilities.

There was a clear synergy between the Olympic and Paralympic Equestrian teams. In September, when the Paralympic Games were taking place, members of the Olympic team competing at the Burghley Horse Trials were kept up to date with progress at the Games. Like other sports – Cycling, Sailing, Athletics, Rowing – the two teams worked from an integrated Olympic/Paralympic programme. Leading the charge, at the forefront of changing perception and infusing the squad with a very individual brilliance, dynamism, creativity and control, were Rio and Sophie. A team within a team, they won their three gold medals in perfect harmony – musical, mathematical and majestic.

Crowning the 'King of Kool'

Brendan Gallagher

Bradley Wiggins seals his momentous sporting summer with a magnificent Time Trial gold

The London 2012 Olympic and Paralympic Games were possibly the most photographed and visual in history. The single picture that has seared itself into my mind, though, is the wonderfully appropriate, slightly bizarre image of Bradley Wiggins after his victory in the men's Time Trial, acknowledging his subjects from an over-sized throne outside Hampton Court Palace. To a degree it was Pythonesque, but such British humour was one of the great attractions of London 2012, a lack of pomposity that brought the Games closer to the people. And Wiggins above all others was the people's champion, the London larrikin and Modfather who made good.

The concept of 'hot seats' near the finish is customary at any major time trial. As the race continues through the day, the top three riders are placed there, remaining until they are replaced by faster competitors. These seats may be sofas or lounge seats; occasionally they are stools, and at one stage old-fashioned bean bags were all the rage, but never before have they been full-blown theatrical thrones, an inspired touch typical of London 2012 and a homage to the Royal Palace venue. Strictly speaking

Wiggins, riding second last ahead of reigning champion Fabian Cancellera of Switzerland, was not required to sit on any of the thrones. Taking the lead at that stage of the race, he could expect to be directed straight from the finish line to the Victory Ceremony and podium in front of Hampton Court Palace after his winning ride. But the world's media were not to be denied. There was a throne and the new King of Cycling needed to be crowned.

Wiggins, rather to his surprise, had become the biggest name in the sport and for a few days, until Sir Chris Hoy caught him up, he was the most decorated British Olympian in history. So, rather warily you sensed, he inched his way towards the throne. The champion's Lennonesque 'V' signs, seeming to signify love and peace as much as victory, combined with a distinct look of bewilderment from the man himself as he posed briefly for the photographers. Many had been eyeing up this opportunity since they had arrived at the Royal Palace shortly after dawn. There was no escape, nor were there any trumpet fanfares or royal proclamations – just the distant chant of 'Wiggo, Wiggo' from the massive crowds still gathered outside the Palace courtyard. As the coronation was completed he could briefly reflect on possibly the most extraordinary and tumultuous month ever experienced by a British competitor from any sport. His life had changed forever.

Wiggins, although a big name within cycling, was relatively unknown to the wider British sporting public. Even a month before the Games started he could undoubtedly have walked down any high street unnoticed and unmolested. But the Tour de France changed that. For three weeks Wiggins, having trained like never before, captivated the nation as he rode the race of his life, becoming the first Briton to win the Tour de France. On the day of his return the national press gave him blanket coverage, leaping beyond the sports sections to embrace the main news pages as well. Suddenly Bradley Wiggins wasn't just the biggest name in British sport – he was the biggest name in Britain itself.

This wasn't an easy situation for any competitor with the Olympic Games now rapidly heaving into view. After riding nearly 36,000km in three weeks he needed to prepare, or recover to be precise, very carefully indeed for the impending Road Race and the Time Trial. For a couple of days Wiggins disappeared back home to Eccleston in Lancashire. He took his son Ben to a Wigan Warriors training camp before travelling to Team GB's hotel and training camp in Surrey.

Mentally Wiggins somehow had to park the winning of the Tour de France, possibly the biggest individual prize in all sport, on a shelf for a week or two. The Olympic Games were just days away, a home Games offering real possibilities for success, but his mind was still gradually processing everything that occurred on the Tour. There were frequent flashbacks as he trained and rested with his Team GB colleagues. At the pre-Olympic Games press conference on 26 July, just two days before the men's Road Race and just three and half days after his triumph in Paris, many of the questions were still focused on the Tour.

Wiggins also had to manage expectations, not least by spelling out to new cycling fans that he wasn't actually a contender in the Olympic Road Race. The cyclists of Team GB would be working exclusively for Mark Cavendish, endeavouring to manufacture – rather against the odds on a hilly course that wasn't ideal for Cavendish – a sprint finish down The Mall. Flushed with Wiggins' Tour de France success there was expectation of a 'certain gold medal', when Cavendish was never more than a reasonable prospect in this most unpredictable cycle race. Favourites seldom take gold in the Olympic Road Race.

Before the race, however, Wiggins had another surprise. Sensing the moment the London Organising Committee of the Olympic and Paralympic Games, LOCOG, got in touch to ask if Wiggins could ring the Olympic Bell at 9pm to signify the start of the Olympic Opening Ceremony. Why not? Team GB had moved up to a central London hotel on Friday for the start of the Road Race and a courier bike was organised. It would all be over in an hour or so. And so, resplendent in his specially produced yellow polo shirt, Wiggins appeared on the stage and did the honours, before an audience of millions. Half an hour later he was back in his hotel room again. A slightly weird experience, to be sure, but when you reach a certain level of fame life is full of such moments.

And so the day of the Road Race arrived. In the event, as some had feared, it proved uncontrollable for Team GB – despite the best efforts of Wiggins, Dave Millar, Chris Froome and Ian Stannard, unable to enlist support from other teams. In truth, why would another team assist Great Britain to produce a sprint finish which Cavendish, nine times out of ten, would win hands down? The Road Race proved a hugely exciting occasion nonetheless. The action was free to view on the roadside, apart from small ticketed areas on Box Hill and The Mall, and after the excitement of the Opening Ceremony the previous evening Britain was ready to party. Surrey Police estimated that well over a million spectators lined the roads for the race, relishing the sense of the Olympic Games proper getting under way. Large screens relayed the action around the route and a carnival atmosphere swiftly arose, with all the roadside barbecues and partying associated with a big stage on the Tour itself.

This was also the first opportunity to pay public homage to Britain's first ever Tour de France winner. The man himself rode flat out in support of Cavendish until 5km from the finish, when it became evident it was a lost cause. From that moment Wiggins turned his full attention to the Time Trial which, if he won, would be his fourth Olympic gold medal and seventh in total. He had three full days recovery back at the Surrey hotel that, as he rightly observed, was practically a holiday after the demands of the Tour de France. His comment that riding in a 44km Time Trial would be a 'doddle' in comparison was slightly misinterpreted as an expectation of easy victory, something Wiggins never thought for a minute.

But he was undeniably in a good place. Going into the Olympic Time Trial, Wiggins had won all six of those in which he had competed during 2012, and he approached such tests against the clock with the confidence of one who hopes to win. Naturally gifted at the event – which involves speed, endurance and the ability to measure your effort – Wiggins had nonetheless made radical changes to his whole approach in the months leading up to the Olympic Time Trial. Such an overhaul, taking place relatively late in his career, dated back to the world championships in Denmark in September 2011. At this event Wiggins, despite winning the silver medal in the Time Trial, was dismayed to finish a full one minute and 20 seconds behind Germany's Tony Martin. Even more frustrating was the discovery that when he and coach Tim Kerrsion analysed the data, it showed that Wiggins and Martin has expended almost exactly the same output. So why was Martin going so much quicker?

It was time for a rethink. Firstly coach Tim Kerrison suggested that Wiggins start working on his core muscles in the gym, never his favourite habitat, because those muscles are vital in fixing a rider's position on the bike and transferring the power through to the pedals and wheels. Then Kerrison suggested that they lower Wiggins' pedal cadence, the speed at which he pushed the pedals, from 105 rpm to 90, and simultaneously introduce a bigger gear. Known within cycling circles as the Jan Ullrich technique, this can only be contemplated by a powerful athlete on top of his or her game. It was in fact the technique the powerful Martin was also using.

The final ingredient was an important shift in mindset. Wiggins by nature is an aggressive time trial rider and prior to 2012, if he had a fault, it was that he went out too quickly and faded slightly at the end. He never 'blew up' and had recorded some fine wins doing it his way, but Kerrison believed a simple change of tactics would improve him. Ideally a rider should cover the second half of the race just as quickly as the first half, automatically ensuring an even distribution of the overall effort, but Wiggins in 2012 started moving that on further. In his pomp Wiggins was now covering the second half of the race even quicker – recording 'negative splits', to use the coaches' jargon. Only a rider with supreme fitness and unflinchable confidence can ride a long time trial in this way, but get it right and you are virtually unbeatable.

This was precisely what happened on the Olympic Time Trial course. Wiggins was simply unstoppable. He started relatively quietly, although still humming along beautifully, and trailed Martin by five seconds at the first checkpoint, after 8km. By the second checkpoint, at 18km, that gap had reduced to just one second, and thereafter it was

Wiggins all the way, gathering pace and momentum as was the plan. By the final checkpoint on Esher High Street he was 23 seconds to the good. Despite taking it very carefully in the final 5km to avoid any unnecessary risks, he came home 44 seconds ahead of silver medal winner Martin, with Great Britain's Froome winning a popular bronze.

Wiggins in full flow on his time trial bike is a sight to behold and the massive crowd enjoyed every last second. Putting aside the technicalities of competitive cycling for a moment, Wiggins is possibly the most stylish bike rider since Fausto Coppi of Italy, one of the reasons why he is revered on the continent. His apparently effortless fluid style, aesthetically beautiful as well as efficient, is always seen to best advantage in the time trial.

Aerodynamically Wiggins is perfect with a back so flat, strong and horizonatal that you could safely serve afternoon tea on it. To help achieve that position he stretches his long arms out on his tri-bars, revealing the letter B, initial of his children Ben and Bella, tattooed on the visible part of each thumb. When he rides, he rides for them and his wife Cath. With elbows tightly tucked in and streamlined, Wiggins' body knows the optimum position from years and years riding with the GB Team Pursuit squad. His head is as motionless as it is possible to be when you are riding a bike at 55kph or more. The only movement you see are those long thin legs, spinning effortlessly.

His position contrasts with two of his main rivals. Taylor Phinney is a mighty athlete and might one day claim an Olympic title, but when time trialling he resembles a nodding donkey, his head regularly ducking in the process of breathing. Meanwhile the splendid, action-packed Froome can look like a teenager riding a motorbike for the first time, appearing on the verge of losing control. Every rider has his or her individual style, but if you are looking for a classic style to copy Wiggins is your man every time.

Relentlessly, beautifully, he homed in on his fourth Olympic gold medal. 'Here Wiggo,' proclaimed some of the banners in the crowd, which included some stylish individuals sporting cutout sideburns offered by two newspapers that very morning. Where had these crowds come from? Britain's sporting public seemed to have suddenly, passionately embraced cycling, with all its sometimes confusing idiosyncracies. Just a couple of days before, on a dark and wet British summer afternoon, they had also flocked to the roadside to support Lizzie Armitstead and the GB women's team as they set out in search of gold. The lightning bolts danced around London and the heavens opened in the Surrey countryside beyond. Yet nothing could take away from the pleasure and drama of the closing stages as Armitstead battled her way through torrential rain on The Mall to a magnificent silver medal, a just reward for a brave and intelligent race. That had been Britain's first medal of the 2012 Olympic Games.

On this golden Wednesday spectators had returned in force, relishing the delicious inevitability of victory. Great Britain, strange to relate, had still won only one of the 29 gold medals they were to claim. The need to celebrate hung heavily in the air, creating a gala occasion that transcended the winning of an Olympic Time Trial title. This was a national event. As Wiggins closed in on the line everybody started banging the boarded section of the barriers in unison – always a spine-tingling moment, but doubly so when it was a British crowd celebrating a British Olympic champion at the London 2012 Olympic Games. The scent of success was heady. The 'King of Kool', the King of Cycling, was about to receive his crown.

Over the Rainbow

Shelagh Fogarty

An amazing haul of gold, silver and bronze medals sees Ellie Simmonds' dreams of Paralympic glory come true at London 2012

'Will you be interviewing Ellie Simmonds?' was the only thing my 10-year-old niece, Grace, wanted to know when she found out I was covering the London 2012 Paralympic Games. Aged just thirteen, Ellie became an instant star after winning double gold in the Swimming 100m – S6 and 400m – S6 races at Beijing 2008. What might this young swimmer, the youngest athlete to compete at the Beijing 2008 Paralympic Games, achieve at a home Games, we wondered. That was soon answered. If Simmonds had been a firework at Beijing, she was a one-woman laser display in London. Two golds, a silver and a bronze, with world records and personal bests dished out like sweets to the 17,500 spectators who filled the Aquatics Centre every day.

I was tantalisingly close to, but outside, the pool when Ellie won her first gold medal of London 2012. She demolished the field to retain her 400m Freestyle – S6 gold medal, smashing the world record and seeing off rival Victoria Arlen of the USA. The Briton's megawatt smile afterwards, mingled with a few tears of joy, gave us a foretaste of what was to come.

Next up for Simmonds was the 200m Individual Medley – SM6, and this time I was determined to be there. Marc Woods, who won 12 Paralympic medals in the pool in his time, four of them gold, broadcast with me every day. He gave me precise instructions for the quickest way to get myself poolside to see this tiny powerhouse attempt to win a second gold in front of a home crowd in full song. Daily cheers burst though the concrete walls of the Aquatics Centre from morning until night, the perfect accompaniment for spectators entering or leaving the Olympic Park.

My work done, and in blistering sunshine, I ran through the crowd in a manner as far removed from an athlete as it's possible to be – panting, hot, bag swinging and work folders ready to spill their contents. I went through the press gate unhindered, only to discover I didn't have a clue where to go from there. Every time a huge roar went up I thought it might be for Ellie and had visions of her touching the wall at the end of her race, first or last, just as I finally walked into that turquoise dream. But I needn't have worried. After a few wrong turns I was put right by those angels of London 2012, the Games Makers, and found myself staring at the Olympic Pool just below the bank of journalists primed to commentate on the race.

And then it happened. A bone-shaking roar erupted as the announcer declared Simmonds' name over the pool tannoy. She waved, smiled, and then got down to business. In the heats she'd knocked 1.17 off her own world mark. 'Oh gosh!' had been her reaction. So what would she deliver now?

It is worth pausing for a moment to explore the numerous classifications in Paralympic Swimming. The athletes are rated from one through to 14: the lower the number, the more severe the impairment. This means someone with Ellie's condition, dwarfism, can be expected to swim alongside a much taller athlete. It's the athletes' ability in the water that is deemed comparable, not their physical shape, height, condition, and so on. So the mixed strokes of the Individual Medley (the 'M' in SM6) means that there can be big variations in an athlete's position at any one time during the race. When Ellie swims alongside a willowy competitor with a more typical swimmer's frame, for example, it can look unfair during the butterfly leg as the rival steams ahead, but that is because she may only be able to use her arms. Once the freestyle leg begins, a huge kicker and finisher such as Ellie can make up apparently lost ground. It gives enthusiastic spectators a tense and nervous time, though.

So back to the 200m Individual Medley – SM6. Back to the sound chamber that is the Aquatics Centre – the loudest assault my eardrums have ever experienced. Unlike the Olympic Stadium it has a roof, so the noise has nowhere to go but inside you. Fifth after the butterfly leg, Simmonds climbed into fourth after the backstroke, still nearly five seconds behind Oksana Khrul of the Ukraine. As the swimmers turned for the final freestyle leg, the Briton was in second place. She accelerated, her powerful arms driving her past Kruhl, overtaken by this onslaught in half a length. For a moment the rest of the field seemed to be sliding backwards in a different pool to the one Simmonds was in. She touched the wall some 25m clear in a new record time of 3.05.39.

We could not cheer any louder, but we tried nonetheless. Gold again! Anyone arriving at the Olympic Park from Stratford station that evening would have been knocked sideways by the wall of sound that greeted them, as if to say 'Welcome to Ellie's world; hope you enjoy your stay!' Still only 17, she has an amazing power to inspire. When I asked my niece why she was so interested in Ellie Simmonds she explained it was because a girl in her class at school has dwarfism too. This girl also loves swimming and, most of all, loves Ellie too – just like the rest of us.

The tears of joy and relief that had followed Simmonds' first medal were nowhere to be seen. She had lit the blue touchpaper in that first golden final; this one was simply to be relished. The Aquatics Centre is 'her place', she joked after the Prime Minister had given her the gold medal – reminding us that, as Britain's youngest MBE, she had already visited Downing Street. When I left the Park an hour or so later, every single person I passed wanted to know if I'd seen Ellie Simmonds win, as though it were some kind of lottery win. It is. To be present when one of Britain's sporting greats is in action at such an inspiring Paralympic Games is quite simply like winning first prize – something that Simmonds knows all about.

We began to expect the gold rush to continue in her other races – the 50m Freestyle – S6 and the 100m Freestyle – S6. She describes the 100 as 'the race that made me the person I am in Beijing', so all hearts were set on her retaining her Olympic crown in this distance. She truthfully played down expectations in interviews she did in the lead-up to the 50m event, explaining, with patient smiles, that she probably wouldn't take a medal in this one. She was serious, her small stature proving a big disadvantage in short-distance races. Taller opponents get a better start simply by being able to propel themselves further, diving long into the pool. Historically Ellie has been an explosive finisher, but racing over such a short distance as 50m gives her little time to make up ground.

Despite her pragmatism in not expecting a medal, she proceeded to win one anyway. Simmonds took bronze and looked ecstatic when she realised she was going to be up where she belongs – on the podium at a home Games, in front of an adoring crowd.

Simmonds' beautiful rivalry with the American swimmer Victoria Arlen gave the spectators even more to relish. I say 'beautiful' because it's how Ellie speaks of it, revealing a genuine affection and respect between the two young women. Their routes to the same pool and the same race couldn't be more different. Ellie was born as she is, but Victoria was paralysed by a virus that affected her spinal column and she spent some years in a vegetative state.

When it looked as though Arlen might not be racing in the same classification group, we knew we'd be missing out on one of sport's great head-to-heads. But that had been averted, and here they both were, the tall American and the tiny Briton, on their marks at the start of the 100m Freestyle – S6. The crowd held their collective breath. Unlike the 50m Ellie would have that second length of the pool to garner momentum with that fabulous kick of hers. Arlen, though, has those long lean swimmer's arms to work with, but no kick of course.

Arlen was still in the lead with just seconds to go. Simmonds simply put her head down in the last 15m and kicked like fury. She swam a personal best, but it wasn't enough to beat off the American, who did a phenomenal swim in a world record time of 1.13.33. The two women hugged in the water, class acts both. Later Simmonds said she was 'gutted' to have lost her beloved Beijing 100m gold, but she still gave all credit to Arlen, saying her swim had been 'unbelievable'.

Moments such as this show the true nature of Ellie

Simmonds. It's easy to beam a smile around the world when you win gold, and what a smile hers is, but she is also extremely sporting when victory eludes her. Simmonds' joy at the unexpected bronze in the 50m counterpoints her phlegmatic acceptance that, despite swimming a personal best time in the 100m, there was someone in the pool on the day whose best was just a little better. She may have lost her Paralympic title, but her integrity is untouched. That's why Simmonds is such a superstar, why children are wild about her. She knows how to behave, but always looks like she's having fun. 'I've got high expectations of myself,' she has quietly observed. 'I'm quite a competitive person and I hate losing.' She does her very best so can accept what comes because she couldn't have done more.

During the years between Beijing 2008 and London 2012 this young woman has gone through puberty, removed her dental braces and honed her sport to an unbelievable level – all under a media spotlight every bit as intense as Jessica Ennis's. When she and other Paralympians turned out in Trafalgar Square one hundred days before the Games began, it was Ellie Simmonds who was swamped by schoolchildren and journalists alike.

Born with achondroplasia or dwarfism, Simmonds began swimming aged four and entered her first competition just a few years later. After watching the Athens 2004 Paralympic Games on television, she was inspired to take her sport to an elite level and stepped up her training with the aim of qualifying for Beijing 2008. In a sport where people have come to expect long, lean limbs, Simmonds' dwarfism is increasingly far down the list of things to say about her. She has charisma by the bucket-load and is at ease with herself. Back in March, at the unveiling of Stella McCartney's kit for the British Olympic and Paralympic teams, Simmonds was chosen to stand alongside Phillips Idowu and Jessica Ennis as the model for the Paralympic livery. During the Games her father commented that her family simply see Ellie as a supremely committed swimmer who plainly loves to perform.

As for her competitiveness, you sensed her sincerity when she welcomed the fact that arch-rival Victoria Arlen would, after all, be allowed to swim in the same races as her. Arlen's strength in the water just spurs me on, was Ellie's message – no secret relief that a tough competitor would bother her no more. Where's the fun in a lost challenge? To someone as bold and dedicated as Ellie Simmonds, none at all.

Simmonds' achievements have had a major impact on Paralympic Swimming, which is already being felt. Even as she powered to those victories four years ago, another young woman was deciding, there and then, to try and become a Paralympic swimmer. Inspired by a girl only just in senior school, Susie Rodgers went on to compete at the 2012 Games. She took three bronze medals in 100m Freestyle – S7, the 4 x 100m Freestyle Relay – 34 points and the 400m Freestyle – S7. The 400m Freestyle medal was to be ParalympicsGB's 100th medal of the London 2012 Paralympic Games – another golden legacy for a remarkable Swimming team. And perhaps my niece's classmate will join them at Rio in four years time.

▲ **14** Jessica Ennis shares with the crowd her delight at taking the gold medal in the Heptathlon. She delivered an outstanding performance across all seven elements, despite the weight of expectation at her home Games.

▲ **15** Captain Kate Walsh (left) is challenged by New Zealand's Cathryn Finlayson during the women's Hockey bronze medal match. Walsh, determined to return after a serious jaw injury, led her team to the bronze medal.

▼ **16** 'So chuffed': Paralympic Cyclist Aileen McGlynn (left) and pilot Helen Scott relish their success in taking bronze in the Pursuit – B. It was their second medal of the Games, following a silver in the 1km Time Trial – B.

17 David Weir (centre) speeds towards his second gold medal of London 2012 in the 1500m – T54. Showing poise, power and tactical skill, the great wheelchair racer took an incredible four gold medals at the Paralympic Games.

18 Ben Ainslie, confirmed as the greatest Olympic sailor of all time, celebrates his fourth gold medal. The champion drew on deep resilience and competitive skill to overcome a slow start to the regatta.

▲ **19** Calm and collected, Sophie Christiansen and her horse Janeiro 6 perform the Freestyle Test: Individual – Grade 1a in the handsome Greenwich Park arena. Her innovative repertoire delighted the crowd and brought her a third gold medal from the Games, each won with exceptional scores of over 80.

◀ **20** On 'Super Saturday', 11 August 2012, Mo Farah grasps the enormity of his achievement after winning the 10,000m final. His was the first-ever British Olympic gold medal at the distance. A week later Farah also took the 5000m, securing the elusive 'double gold' to join an exclusive band of athletes.

▲ **21** Team GB's Bradley Wiggins relaxes on a Hampton Court Palace 'throne' following victory in the men's Time Trial. Only weeks after winning the Tour de France, he proved unstoppable on the Olympic course, taking the gold medal by 44 seconds in front of an ecstatic crowd.

▲ **22** Deafening cheers from spectators drive Ellie Simmonds forward to victory in the 200m Individual Medley – SM6. Still only 17, the Paralympic swimmer set a new record time to take her second gold, and third medal, of her home Games before a jubilant Aquatics Centre crowd.

◀ **23** Usain Bolt silences the doubters as he storms to his second successive 100m Olympic gold medal. Despite rumours about his fitness and the challenge of rivals prior to the Games, the Jamaican proved himself at London 2012 to be the greatest sprinter in the world.

▲ **24** ParalympicsGB's Sarah Storey dominates the field of the women's Road Race – C4/5 at Brands Hatch. She won the race to take her fourth gold of London 2012, bringing her overall tally to 11, level with Tanni Grey-Thompson and swimmer David Roberts – a feat Storey describes as 'immense'.

▶ **25** Sir Chris Hoy is overcome with emotion as he receives his gold medal for the men's Keirin. The 36-year-old, the most successful British Olympian of all time with six gold medals, described it as the 'perfect end' to his Olympic career.

▲ **26** ParalympicsGB's rising star Jonnie Peacock roars in delight as he crosses the line to take gold in the 100m – T44. The teenager overcame both defending champion Oscar Pistorius and Brazil's Alan Oliveira in the final. South Africa's Arnu Fourie (left) took the bronze medal.

The Best There's Ever Been

Tom Knight

Usain Bolt defies fitness rumours to seize a historic double-double gold

There had been questions about Usain Bolt's form and fitness going into the Olympic Games. Answers were to come after just 50m of the final when, having recovered from a shaky start, the big man's body was upright, his arms were pumping and he drifted past Justin Gatlin on his inside to put daylight between him and the world's finest sprinters.

We knew then that Bolt the magnificent, Bolt the world-beater, Bolt the wannabe legend was back. In the blink of an eye the athlete who won three gold medals in such sensational style at Beijing 2008 had shown that the intrigue and drama surrounding his fitness that dominated headlines in the preceding weeks was over. After his customary 41 strides and with a healthy following wind of 1.5m/sec, Bolt swept through the finish line with an exaggerated dip. He stopped the clock at 9.63, an Olympic record and the second quickest time in history. Only he had run faster.

And what of Yohan Blake, his Jamaican teammate, training partner and the youngest-ever world champion after Bolt's disqualification for a false start in Daegu in 2011? Where was the young pretender who had twice beaten Bolt so convincingly over 100m and 200m only five weeks before at their national Olympic trials? Was not the 22-year-old Blake supposed to succeed Bolt as the Olympic champion? There were plenty of journalists, track and field enthusiasts and bookmakers who thought so.

We knew at 50m that this was not the scenario about to enfold. As Bolt was hitting full speed, finding top gear and looking good, Blake was straining to keep his place in the pack. The race for the gold medal was over from that moment onwards.

'My coach told me after the trials not to worry about my start,' Bolt explained. 'For me it was just about reacting and executing my first 30m because my last 50m is the best part of my race. At 50m I was with the crowd and I knew I was going to win after that so I just ran my hardest.' So confident of victory was he that Bolt claimed that he *almost* repeated the showboating that made his Beijing 2008 triumph so popular but – four years older and wiser – he thought better of it.

Blake, whose youthful grin and high-pitched voice rather belies his self-imposed moniker of 'The Beast', won the battle for the silver medal and equalled his personal best of 9.75 – ironically the same time that had been enough for victory at the trials. There probably lay the reason for what enfolded on that magical night in London's Olympic Stadium. As for Gatlin, the American who won this title in 2004 but then served a four-year ban for his second doping offence, he took the bronze medal in 9.79, a personal best.

Behind the medallists the two other Americans, Tyson Gay and Ryan Bailey, came fourth and fifth. Churandy Martina of the Netherlands was sixth and Trinidad and Tobago's Richard Thompson seventh. All of them recorded times of less than 10 seconds. The only finalist to miss that distinction was Asafa Powell. The unfortunate Jamaican suffered a hamstring injury and jogged across the line a long way back in 11.99.

Bolt had secured his place in history as the first sprinter to cross the line first in successive Olympic 100m finals. He kept on running to 150m before stopping to kiss the track and perform his traditional lightning bolt stance for the 80,000 lucky ticket-holders still applauding what they had just seen. Given that the previous evening had produced an extraordinary three British gold medallists within the space of 45 minutes, the men's 100m had a lot to live up to, but Bolt had delivered.

Celebrations erupted throughout the Jamaican community in London and in the country's capital, Kingston. Here, despite the onset of tropical storm Ernesto, fans took to the streets to dance and sing Bolt's praises. The Jamaican gold and silver in the men's 100m, together with the gold and bronze won by Shelly-Ann Fraser-Pryce and Veronica Campbell-Brown in the women's sprint on Saturday night, simply added to the party atmosphere surrounding the 50th anniversary of Jamaica's independence.

As for Bolt, he knew he could – and would – deliver a gold medal-winning performance a lot sooner than those watching in the Olympic Stadium or on television. He suggested as much after his semi-final when he cantered through the line, easing up in 9.87, ahead of Bailey. He waved his forefinger in an 'I told you so' riposte to all those who doubted him coming into the Games.

Yet Bolt himself was partly responsible for those doubts. He had been beaten twice in the space of three days by Blake at the end of June, and after the 200m had received treatment for a hamstring problem. He pulled out of a race in Monaco later in July that was to have been his last before the Olympic Games, with his coach, Glen Mills, citing an injury that needed treatment, without offering any further details.

So the speculation flowed, and that is all it ever was. Bolt arrived in the UK with the rest of the Jamaican Athletics squad and took up residence at the team holding camp in Birmingham, but was never prepared to train at the Alexander Stadium while any cameras were present. The intrigue intensified; media flights of fantasy took hold in the vacuum presented by Bolt and Mills. As the Games drew nearer, Bolt told the BBC that he was '95 per cent fit' and finally, at a packed and overly orches-trated press conference in a former brewery warehouse in Whitechapel, he answered a direct question about his form and fitness. 'I had a slight problem, but nothing too serious,' he admitted. 'I got that fixed. I'm ready to go. It's all about the championships, not the trials.'

Those who had followed Bolt's career knew that he had problems with his back and hamstrings ever since he emerged as a teenage sensation in Jamaica. Still a month shy of his 16th birthday, he became the youngest ever winner of the world junior 200m title, receiving the Rising Star award in 2002 and 2003 from the International Association of Athletics Federations. He suffered ham-string problems in 2003 and in 2004, however, when he did not qualify from his heat at the Athens 2004 Olympic Games.

Clearly what became apparent at the Jamaican Olympic trials in 2012 was that Bolt was not as fit as he should have been, but he still had five weeks to put things right. Blake, on the other hand, was at the top of his game – possibly too early in the season. Bolt spent the next five weeks wisely, getting specialist treatment for his trouble-some hamstring and back and plenty of massages and physiotherapy. There was training too, to top up the speed endurance that was lacking at the trials. Ricky Simms, his British agent, said that Bolt never needed long to improve in training, but the trials had been a timely reminder that the work had to be done.

The result was that Bolt arrived at the Olympic Village in London knowing he was in much better shape than he had been. Blake could not have had such confidence. The wagging finger after his semi-final was Bolt reassuring himself as well as the crowd that all was well, and so it proved in the final.

He was not the first to retain his Olympic 100m title. Carl Lewis did that, at Los Angeles 1984 and Seoul 1988. In Seoul it was by default when the race winner Ben Johnson tested positive for a banned steroid and was disqualified.

It is interesting nonetheless to put some historical per-spective on what Bolt achieved in London. Many have tried to retain the Olympic 100m title, including the Soviet sprinter Valerie Borzov. He dominated the event at Munich 1972 and won the gold medal in 10.14. When he clocked the same time in Montreal four years later, it placed him third behind the winner Hasely Crawford from Trinidad and Tobago. Britain's Linford Christie triumphed at Barcelona 1992, but was nowhere near the same ath-lete in Atlanta, where he was disqualified for a false start in the final. Another American, Maurice Greene, was the champion at Sydney 2000 with a time of 9.87. However, at Athens – like Borzov – he ran exactly the same and finished third, with the gold medal going to Gatlin.

The four years between Olympic Games has so often been too much for athletes to bridge, and yet Bolt had come through his biggest test. Commentating on television, the two-time Olympic 400m champion Michael Johnson called Bolt 'the best there's ever been', and few would disagree with that assessment.

It was not enough for Bolt though. At 25, the 6ft 5in sprinting phenomenon, the son of a grocer from the farming community of Trelawny, whose earliest love was cricket, decided that he wanted to be a *legend*. It was as if being the greatest sprinter of all time was not quite enough. 'Becoming a legend is my ultimate goal,' he told anyone who asked. 'That's my goal right there. That means defending my titles.'

That meant the 200m in a couple of days' time and the 4 x 100m Relay at the end of what would be a punishing week. Yet it didn't take Bolt long to revert to his partying self … or so it seemed. A snapshot of the new Olympic champion surrounded by three beautiful women was posted on Twitter at 3am the following morning. Not all was what it seemed, however, as he happily explained. Unable to sleep after his momentous victory, he had gone looking for food in the huge canteen at the Olympic Village, and had run into three members of the Swedish Handball team.

Bolt switched his focus to the 200m, his favourite event, but nothing was certain. To retain the 100m had been an amazing achievement; could he really achieve the 200m as well? It had never been done – not even by Carl Lewis, who, interestingly, was beaten in the 200m at Seoul 1988 by his much younger training partner, Joe DeLoach. On paper, the 200m gave Blake the chance to avenge his defeat in the 100m and, once again, threw up questions about Bolt's stamina for the long haul. His start was again under the microscope.

Bolt's response? He led from the turn and crossed the line in 19.32, matching the time many believed would stand for decades when Michael Johnson set it as a world record when he won this race in 1996. It was 0.02 off the Olympic record Bolt ran in 2008, but still too good for Blake. He was closer, certainly, but still more than a tenth of a second adrift in taking silver. Bolt later admitted that he had felt a strain in his back coming off the curve. 'The key thing was always run the corner as fast as possible because I know I am a better turn runner than Yohan. I think I ran it a little too fast as, when I came off, I could feel a slight strain in my back so I decided I was going to keep my eyes on him and make sure I stayed in front. I did just that, and that's the reason I slowed down at the line.'

This was Bolt being cautious, but he still had the foresight to put a forefinger to his lips in his moment of triumph. 'That was for all the doubters,' he said, perhaps stating the obvious. 'I was telling people I was going to win and I was going to make myself a legend. That was just for them, to tell them "you can stop talking now, I'm a living legend". People were doubting me. After the trials there were a lot of people doubting me, but that is good because you know who your true friends are. In Jamaica we call them *wagonists*, so for me it was great to really come out and show the world and show my true fans that I am the best.'

As entertaining as ever in front of the massed media, Bolt showed no sign of modesty in marking his historic double-double. 'I am now a living legend. Bask in my glory,' he declared with a smile. A bronze medal for Warren Weir made it a Jamaican clean sweep and the Olympic Stadium erupted once again to the sight of Bolt and Blake playing up to the cameras. The glorious mix of sporting excellence and showmanship was intoxicating, even for a crowd now accustomed to the wonders unfolding in that Olympic Stadium. Suffice to say that Bolt even managed to upstage David Rudisha, the eloquent, quietly spoken Kenyan who earlier in the evening had produced probably the performance of the Olympic Games to smash the world record in the 800m.

The 4 x 100m Relay provided Bolt, Blake and the rest of the Jamaican squad with the opportunity to sign off with a flourish. They did not disappoint. As defending champions and winners of the previous two world championship titles, the Jamaicans – Bolt, Blake, Nesta Carter and Michael Frater – were obviously the favourites, but still had to contend with a USA team in cracking form.

The two teams were neck and neck at the final changeover. It was to be Bolt who pulled away from Ryan Bailey in the home stretch to secure the gold medal and the first clocked time under 37 seconds. The Jamaicans had taken the world record they set at the 2011 world championships to 36.84.

Bolt almost blighted his copybook by hanging on to the baton instead of handing it to the official beyond the finish line. He wanted to keep it as a souvenir, but the official insisted that the baton's return meant the completion of the race. There was an exchange of opinions before Bolt relented, only to be presented with it later.

Another world record, a third gold medal in London, a sixth gold medal in total for the self-proclaimed living legend. It was an astonishing way for these Olympic Games to end and yet the 4 x 100m Relay had merely underlined how this four-yearly festival of sport brings out the very best in performance. Bolt's fortune, already estimated to be around $20 million, is set to rocket in the coming years, and in London he toyed with questions about his next challenge, even suggesting that he might turn to the long jump. The Rio 2016 Olympic Games could present him with a challenge he might have trouble resisting, however, despite the increasing demands on his time from an ever-growing roster of sponsors. Those decisions would be left for another day.

According to the former sprinter from Trinidad and Tobago Ato Boldon, an Olympic medallist at 100m and 200m, Bolt's place in history is assured. 'Bolt has a knack for not just knowing the moment, but being the moment,' said Boldon. 'In Berlin, at the 2009 world championships, after smashing his own world records in the 100m and 200m, he came out in a shirt that said *ICH BIN EIN BERLINER* and Germans loved it. In London he wins gold number three and does the 'Mobot' to honour the UK's current track star Mo Farah, who had completed a golden double of his own that evening. That sort of thing is unprecedented. Track stars, even mega-track-stars in the past, haven't been able to endear themselves to a whole nation with that sort of immediacy.'

Showman to the end, Bolt lingered in the Olympic Stadium on the final night of Athletics to celebrate with Farah as the Briton received his gold medal for the 5000m. As he began what will surely be long and colourful celebrations of his unique triple-triple, Bolt called it 'a wonderful end to a wonderful week'. He has a way with words as well as sprinting.

Achieving the Impossible ... Again

Brendan Gallagher

Another magnificent seven gold medals at the Velodrome

Many things changed dramatically between 2008 and 2012, a world financial crisis arose for one, but the sight of Sir Chris Hoy leaving a vapour trail on the track and winning gold for Great Britain was a constant. Beijing 2008 closed with the sight of Hoy winning the Keirin in commanding style, and it was the big Scot who brought the curtain down on the Olympic Games in identical fashion – another extraordinary triumph in the same event. Hoy's race, and the manner of his victory, was a thing of wonder, offering just a hint of divine intervention.

Taking on the race from the front in the final two laps, Hoy seemed to be fading. He entered the final bend with the other five riders on his shoulder, poised to spring from his slipstream. But the crowd wouldn't allow it, and neither would he. Hoy clung on to the inside line and engaged that big engine one final time in earnest, while the crowd propelled him along by sheer force of decibels. Somehow he emerged into the home straight still in front and, as he crossed the line, his vanquished opponents yet again shook their heads in disbelief. It was his sixth and final Olympic gold medal, a figure that eased him past Sir Steve Redgrave's total of five, although Hoy immediately dismissed any comparisons. He still considers Redgrave's achievement of winning a gold medal at five consecutive Olympic Games as the ultimate.

Of course, none of this was really meant to happen. Hoy still riding so well at 36 years old to garner Great Britain's seventh Track Cycling gold, equalling their record-breaking achievements at Beijing 2008. But it did, as all of us privileged enough to be trackside will bear witness. The secret? Who knows, but listen to British Cycling programme director Dave Brailsford, in animated form soon after Hoy's last triumph. 'Our team is not a fluffy group of people,' he said, 'we are narky and we have our issues. We are like a family in many respects. We bicker, moan, and it's hard to keep everyone together, but ultimately the team pulled it together when it really matters, like it would do for a family. But through that period you have to push people out of the comfort zone. I know from different personal experiences that unless I'm frightened or scared or something I become lethargic and lazy. The bottom line is that often the fear of losing is a much bigger emotion and motivator than the joy of winning.'

So Brailsford and his team, against the odds, had achieved the impossible again. For the best part of four years many of us who follow the sport had been shaking our heads with a slightly pained resignation. Of course there was no way that Great Britain's cyclists could ever equal the 'Great Haul of China' when, at Beijing 2008, they 'owned' Laoshan Velodrome. Team GB were undeniably brilliant on that occasion, but, to use Brailsford's own phrase, they rode the perfect wave. They suffered no illness, crashes or mechanical failures, nor were there any disqualifications. Great Britain's once-in-a-lifetime squad all fired in unison and the result was truly spectacular.

But London 2012 was always going to be different. Indeed, it was designed specifically to be so by the International Olympic Committee (IOC) and the International Cycling Union (UCI) who wanted to be more inclusive of other Cycling nations. Reluctant to have any one nation take such a grip of its Track Cycling programme, they had introduced a raft of changes. From now on there would be just one competitor per country in the individual events. This meant no more doubling up for Team GB in their strongest events. Particularly affected were the men's Sprint and men's Keirin, in both of which Great Britain took gold and silver at Beijing 2008. It was a bit like Jamaica or the USA having to nominate just one runner in the men's 100m.

The UCI also decided to dispense with the men's and women's Individual Pursuit. Considered the purest and most traditional of track events, they had seen Bradley Wiggins and Rebecca Romero so dominant at the Beijing 2008 Games. The introduction of the multi-element Omnium event also appeared to work against Great Britain, with that rider having to come from the Team Pursuit squads. Such a stipulation clearly favoured riders from teams who either had no intention, or lacked the ability, to contest the Team Pursuit medals. From Team GB's perspective, the only shaft of sunlight was the introduction of more women's events. The Team Sprint and Keirin at least gave Victoria Pendleton more shots at a medal.

Brailsford, however, remained cool, although in public he started playing down expectations for London 2012. 'No team will ever win seven gold medals on the track again. It cannot be done,' he proclaimed, but privately he and the Team GB coaches weren't so sure. The gauntlet had been thrown down and Brailsford's default setting is always to question those who insist something can't be achieved. 'Why not? Who says so? Where is the data that says we can't do that?' Logically, despite the wide-ranging changes, the strongest and best-prepared nation should still surely prevail. He and his 'think tank' of coaches went to work, and although the results were not immediate, a number of seriously savvy cycling brains – Brailsford, Shane Sutton and Chris Boardman – were ticking over, grappling with the question most waking hours. How exactly do you achieve the impossible twice on the bounce?

First came a long rest, an opportunity to recharge the batteries and explore other projects, not least for Brailsford himself who devoted large chunks of time to starting up Team Sky, the professional cycling team that aimed to win the Tour de France. Team GB track cycling appeared to splutter along a little. Hoy crashed and missed a season, as Geraint Thomas departed for a while to get his road career under way. Jamie Staff was forced to retire through injury and Bradley Wiggins was seen less and less on the boards. It was a time for steady nerves as they threw the youngsters in – Laura Trott, Dani King, Joanna Rowsell, Philip Hindes – but scratch the surface and Team GB were still ticking over very nicely in the Olympic events at the UCI World Championships. In 2010 they secured eight medals, including three gold, in the ten Olympic disciplines. The following year they also garnered eight medals with two gold. The platform was still there.

Then came the coup Brailsford had been planning for a couple of years. With the 2012 World Championships in Melbourne in April, Team GB had to make a big decision regarding tackling the resurgent Australians. Send an understrength squad down and concentrate on training back home? Or arrive in Australia with the 'full monty' and land a few body blows? After some debate they chose the latter. The gamble exceeded all expectations as the British team claimed five gold medals in the Olympic events, a stunning raid from which the Australians never recovered. The rest of the cycling world also looked on in shock. It seemed as though their worst nightmares were about to come true again.

So the scene was set for the opening day at the London Velodrome, one of the fastest and most spectacular tracks in the world. The thermostat was turned up to a sweaty 28°C and the stewards were ordered to keep the doors shut so as not to disturb the airflow. The home crowd started to roar – it's difficult to remember them going quiet at any stage during the six days that followed – and hearts started pounding up in the press seats, never mind down on the track. No other sound throughout the Olympic Games, not even at the main Olympic Stadium itself on a big Athletics night, had quite the electricity and intensity of the Velodrome. The low roof contained and then amplified it tenfold until no other sensation existed, except the noise.

Team GB made their presence known instantly on the first night and you could almost hear the rest of the cycling world groan. Within days L'Equipe was calling it the Poulidor Complex, the resignation that you are destined to finish second at best. French road racer Raymond Poulidor stood on the podium of the Tour de France on eight occasions without once winning the race.

In the women's Team Sprint Victoria Pendleton and Jessica Varnish raced to a world record, later to be disqualified after their semi-final, having seemingly booked a place in the final against China. Meanwhile, in the men's Team Pursuit, Great Britain effortlessly lowered their own world record in qualifying while the Australians, who had dominated them for three years after Beijing 2008, suddenly looked vulnerable and nervous. The much vaunted Boy-Band – all four Ozzies were young, photogenic and gung-ho – suddenly seemed distinctly off tune and lacking maturity. Their dazzling white smiles were replaced with grimaces.

And then came the men's Team Sprint, which, both at the time and in retrospect, was a dagger in the ribs to would-be opponents. Going into the Olympic Games nobody, other than those inside the Team GB camp who had seen them riding at the holding camp in Newport, gave Great Britain the remotest chance of taking gold. Battered from pillar to post for the previous four years by both France and Germany, and even on occasions by Australia, bronze was surely the best they could achieve.

Great Britain had other plans and, in fairness, enjoyed a stroke of luck. In their qualifying heat young Philip Hindes, their talented but rookie 'man one', lurched out of the gate, the victim of either a mechanical fault or a comically bad start. He fell to the ground with a theatrical flourish and the commissar quickly ordered a rerun, a decision that appeared rather generous at the time although no opposition teams protested. It was the rub of the green Great Britain needed. They went again and shook their opponents to the core by qualifying first in 43.065, an Olympic record and their fastest time since Beijing 2008. Then, in the next round, Team GB broke Germany's world record. Finally, for good measure, they broke their own newly established world record again in the final when they routed France in 42.600. En route 'man two', Jason Kenny, and 'man three', Hoy, produced the fastest second and third lap times in history. This meant four Great

British world records in just under three hours. The same thought ran like lightning around the Velodrome: 'Here we go again.'

Not once did Great Britain take their foot off the pedal. When you are in that kind of form success is contagious; it infects everybody. The Velodrome became a place of worship as much as sport, the high altar of British excellence where native attributes of hard work, left-field thinking and a warrior spirit could be celebrated on a nightly basis. The reassurance and feelgood factor that British cycling has brought to Team GB's overall Olympic performance in recent years can never be underestimated. The message, subliminal or otherwise, has been strong. This is how you prepare and this is how you win gold medals. Again and again.

The gold rush was soon under way. The men's Team Pursuit squad of Ed Clancy, Steven Burke, Peter Kennaugh and Geraint Thomas destroyed Australia in the final, helping themselves to yet another world record in the process. Thomas had rashly offered his colleagues a bottle of Cristal champagne for each tenth of a second they took off the world record during the course of the Games; he eventually found himself shelling out for 15 bottles with a retail price of £134.95 to get the party going afterwards. A small price to pay for such a historic ride.

Pendleton, meanwhile, had looked extraordinarily quick during the Team Sprint and, after nearly a decade of proving herself the toughest of opponents, nobody doubted she would come roaring back the next day after the disappointment of disqualification from a faulty change. She fiercely contested the Keirin, not necessarily her favourite event, but a heaven-sent opportunity for immediate redemption. What transpired was stunning. Not once on that hot sweaty Friday did she loose her cool or look remotely like losing. Hers, when it came, was possibly the most routine gold medal of the entire Games.

Except perhaps for the women's Team Pursuit, the hottest favourites of the Track Cycling meeting having broken the world record for their event in their previous three rides. With a splendid sense of symmetry they then broke that record in each of their three rides at the London Velodrome. It was a staggering performance, technically the performance of the entire six-day competition, with their only opponent being the clock. As Laura Trott, Joanna Rowsell and Dani King stood on the podium, having received their gold medals, the crowd spontaneously started singing *Hey Jude*; Sir Paul McCartney, standing in their midst, started to conduct and sing along to his own masterpiece. Perhaps *Ticket to Ride* or a *Hard Day's Night* might have been even more fitting, but nobody cared. It was a 'Happy and Glorious' moment, to borrow both from the national anthem and IOC President Jacques Rogge's summing up of the Games.

And still the gold medals kept coming; Team GB was on the rampage. Jason Kenny had looked in the form of his life from the start, as befits a man who had persuaded the Great British coaches during the summer that he was riding faster, and was a better bet for gold, than Hoy in the individual Sprint. It was a close and fiendishly tough call, but the correct one. The resulting surge in Kenny's confidence was tangible. For four years he had battled with his colleague, friend and 'roomie', and at the end of it he had been preferred to Great Britain's greatest-ever Track Cycling Olympian. Frankly, after that the Olympic Games were a doddle. The quiet man from Bolton had already won his toughest battle. After recording one of the fastest-ever qualifying laps for the flying 200m with a time of 9.713, he crushed every opponent, including France's reigning world champion Grégory Baugé in the final. A nonplussed Baugé interrupted the post-race press conference to ask, in a genuine spirit of baffled enquiry, how Kenny was managing to ride so fast and how Great Britain kept on winning gold medals.

The meeting built towards a remarkable crescendo on the final Tuesday with the ebullient Trott scrapping for gold in the women's Omnium, Hoy bringing the curtain down on his Olympic career in that wondrous Keirin and Pendleton retiring altogether after the women's individual Sprint. There were going to be tears before bedtime. Trott, an exciting all-round talent and the heir apparent to Pendleton's 'Queen of the Track' title, had quickly become a crowd favourite, never more so than the evening before when she had fought her way to victory in the elimination race, the third of the six disciplines that make up the Omnium. On the final day it was neck and neck with Sarah Hammer of the USA, who won the 3km time trial with Trott second and then nicked another point by finishing second to Trott's third in the scratch race. It all came down to the 500m time trial – a speciality of Trott's, but a race in which she needed to finish three places ahead of Hammer to be certain of gold. The crowd started chanting her name before the race, Hoy had a reassuring word and she was off. There was never any doubt that Trott would win the 500m time trial, but Hammer was running second until the final 125m. The gold was Trott's second of the meeting to match the achievement of boyfriend Kenny who had also bagged a pair. The most be-medalled couple of the Games.

And finally to the big two, Pendleton and Hoy, the

bedrocks of British track cycling for so long. Pendleton had looked unstoppable, but in the final against her old rival Anna Meares, it all went strangely wrong. It served as a reminder of the knife-edge all British riders had been treading. True, she 'won' the first heat, but was then relegated for coming off the racing line, which she undoubtedly did on a couple of occasions, although TV evidence also suggested that might have been in reaction to Meares leaning into her with her left elbow. In the second race the magic suddenly deserted her. Pendleton looked hesitant; she couldn't find the surge of pace down the back straight that has been routing all-comers. She glided home in second place and out of track cycling for good. There were tears, but they were tears of goodbye rather than bitterness, and she proclaimed Meares a worthy winner. The two old rivals hugged as true Olympians do.

Some 10 minutes later there were more tears, this time from the hard man of track cycling, as Hoy stood atop the Olympic podium for the last time. The enormity of his achievements hit him full force with wave upon wave of emotion. It was the perfect way to conclude the Olympic Games Track Cycling programme, and in the same instant another thought forced its way into your mind. This can't happen again at Rio 2016, can it? Another seven gold medals for Team GB is impossible surely? Yet stranger things have happened...

A Changing of the Guard

Tom Knight

Jonnie Peacock tops the bill on 'Thrilling Thursday'

It was difficult to see where it originated, but the sound grew louder and gathered momentum until it reverberated around the Olympic Stadium. With the evening's main race about to get under way, it felt as if 80,000 people were rhythmically clapping and chanting 'Peacock, Peacock.'

In the nine Olympic Games I'd been to, this was a first. I'd seen Carl Lewis, Maurice Greene and Usain Bolt run the 100m in the biggest stadia in the world. I'd seen them win gold medals, break world records, but I had never seen anything like this. This was a spontaneous, sustained chant for a 19-year-old British sprinter at the London 2012 Paralympic Games, about to run in the final of the 100m – T44: someone who, two weeks before, had been largely unknown outside his native Cambridgeshire. At around 9.20pm on Thursday 7 September Jonnie Peacock, a good-looking lad with a sweep of blond hair, became a phenomenon – although he had done nothing apart from qualify for this final the evening before.

The noise was too much for the starter, Alan Bell. He asked the athletes to stand and the Stadium announcer asked for quiet. Peacock smiled and turned to the people behind the starting blocks and put his finger to his lips. He smiled sheepishly at the fuss being caused on his behalf.

It was not as if he had been the only one given a rapturous welcome when he had been introduced to the crowd. There was a cheer for China's Zhiming Liu in lane two, a slighter louder one for Alan Oliveira from Brazil in lane three and an almighty roar for Oscar Pistorius, the smiling South African known as the 'Blade Runner' and the most famous Paralympian in the world. Richard Browne from the USA was given a warm welcome, as was Arnu Fourie, another South African, and the final two Americans in the line-up, Blake Leeper in lane eight and Jerome Singleton in lane nine. Singled out, however, from the moment the athletes appeared in the Stadium, was Peacock.

This was a big night for the youngster and it was rapidly turning into a huge occasion for the British team and the Paralympic Games. In the Stadium we had already seen Hannah Cockcroft win her second gold in the women's 200m – T34. Only minutes before David Weir had claimed his third gold medal on the track in the men's 800m – T54. There had been magnificent bronze medals for Ben Rushgrove in the men's 200m – T36 and Paul Blake in the men's 800m – T36. Earlier in the day, Beverley Jones had also won a bronze medal in the Discus Throw – F37. As if that had not been enough, even the 19-year-old Ola Abidogun had claimed a bronze medal in the men's 100m – T46, and he was supposed to have been one for the future. Surely, the word went around, if Ennis, Rutherford and Farah's night of gold medals at the Olympic Games came on 'Super Saturday', then this must be 'Thrilling Thursday'. And still Peacock had not left his blocks. The level of tension inside the Olympic Stadium as the athletes prepared for another start was truly astonishing.

Why? For the uninitiated, up until the beginning of

the Paralympic Games, the men's 100m – T44 was just another race for Pistorius to win. After all, the 'Blade Runner' was the defending champion in the 100m, 200m and 400m – T44 and the poster boy of the Paralympic Games. He had challenged the International Association of Athletics Federations (IAAF) to win the right to compete with non-disabled athletes, and was running so well that he had also contested the 400m at the Olympic Games only a fortnight before.

Peacock, by contrast, was an unheralded 19-year-old who had listed Pistorius as one of his heroes. When he was drawn alongside the 'Blade Runner' at the 2010 World Cup event in Manchester, in his first major race, the 16-year-old Peacock had called it 'an honour' to compete against him. On that occasion, Pistorius was the easy winner and Peacock finished fifth.

Pistorius continued to dominate any discussion on the Paralympic Games. In June 2012 Peacock broke the world record with 10.85 in a race in the USA. While his performance went largely unnoticed in the media, Pistorius understood what it meant – and so did Peacock. Training alongside established internationals such as Greg Rutherford and Christine Ohuruogu at the Lee Valley High Performance Centre in north London, within sight of the Olympic Stadium, he worked under the direction of Dan Pfaff, the American coach who has helped some of the world's top sprinters, including Carl Lewis and Ryan Bailey. Nurtured by Peter Eriksson, the Paralympic Head Coach at UK Athletics, Peacock's confidence increased by leaps and bounds as the Games approached.

On his arrival at the Paralympic Games, Pistorius, now more of a 200m/400m specialist, acknowledged that the 100m – T44 would be difficult. He mentioned Peacock as one of those capable of doing well. It was good PR ahead of the Games to give the Briton a good build-up, after all.

On 2 September, with the Games under way and the Stadium full for every session, we saw the biggest shock of all – Pistorius' aura of invincibility on the track shattered in an extraordinary 200m – T44. With 50m to go, the 'Blade Runner' was away and clear and running strongly. Before the crowd could begin cheering him home, however, Alan Fonteles Cardoso Oliveira, the unfancied Brazilian, mounted what could only be described as a charge from fifth place. A double amputee like Pistorius, also running on carbon-fibre blades, Oliveira romped past the South African to snatch the most unexpected of victories.

Watching from just beyond the finish line, in seats reserved for athletes, was Peacock. He had trained well and honed his preparations at the team's holding camp in Portugal, barely containing his excitement. Seeing Pistorius under pressure only added to Peacock's belief that he could win the gold medal. He could not wait to get on to the track in the Olympic Stadium.

Within minutes of his defeat, Pistorius had used a trackside post-race interview to question the legitimacy of Oliveira's blades. Oliveira had to remind everyone that his blades had passed the pre-Games inspection and the International Paralympic Committee (IPC) confirmed that no rules had been broken. Pistorius had made the Paralympic Games a major talking point around the world, but his well-nurtured image took something of a beating as he appeared in that instant to be a poor loser. Pistorius was quick to apologise, admitting that his comments had been 'distasteful'. He went on to anchor South Africa to victory in the 4 x 100m Relay – T42-46.

Then his attention, and everyone else's, shifted to the

100m – T44. In the heats, it was Peacock who was the fastest qualifier for the final, due to include both Pistorius and Oliveira. Singleton (USA), the silver medallist at Beijing 2008, was expected to be a contender also, but the final was very much about Pistorius, Oliveira and Peacock. The 100m – T44 had become the most eagerly awaited event of the entire Paralympic Games.

That's why the tension was mounting. It rose still further when Oliveira, the only one of the eight finalists not using his blocks, toppled over the line in the 'set' position. The second interruption prompted another outburst of 'Peacock, Peacock' as the crowd wondered if Oliveira's stumble would mean disqualification for a false start. The mood quietened when an official marched across the track brandishing a green card, effectively warning all the athletes to keep their composure for what was rapidly becoming a nervous time for everyone in the Olympic Stadium.

Peacock went onto his blocks for a third time, once again kissing the St Christopher medallion around his neck. The chanting faded and silence reigned. It was so quiet that in the tier above the press tribune we could hear a baby crying. 'Thrilling Thursday' was about to become an evening few would forget.

Bell's gun unleashed a torrent of noise and Peacock was first to rise. Liu, an early challenger, faded just as quickly, with the USA's Browne the only one to offer any resistance to Peacock's powerful sprint to the line. The Briton swept through the finish to stop the clock at 10.90, a Paralympic record. Like Bolt, he kept on sprinting around the curve as television cameras captured his ecstatic reaction. He stopped to stare at the giant screen, waiting for confirmation of what he must surely have already known. When his name appeared as the winner, so Peacock grinned and turned as Pistorius, who had finished only fourth, became the first to congratulate the new champion. Browne, who had taken silver in 11.03, was next. Dan Greaves, his Great Britain teammate who was only halfway through his Shot Put competition, ran across the infield to give Peacock a hug. The Union flags waved, the chants of 'Peacock, Peacock' began again and photographers clicked away as they tried to track the gold medallist on his lap of honour.

He ran into the back straight and there, in the front row of seats, was his mother, Linda. It was an emotional moment as Peacock sought her out and gave her the biggest hug of all. Her son, who lost his right leg to meningitis at the age of five and who had hopped his way through the school sports day when he was six and ballet classes when he was seven, was the Paralympic champion. His 100m – T44 victory, watched by more than six million viewers in the UK, had made Peacock the star of 'Thrilling Thursday', a national sensation in the most popular sporting action of the Paralympic Games. Four years before, when the Games took place in Beijing, Peacock did not even know that races for people like him existed. He had still to attend the British Paralympic Association (BPA) talent identification day that was to change his life.

The excitement, the tension, the reaction – everything about that night took Peacock and the rest of us by surprise. 'The build-up to this race has been huge and the crowd was surreal … I had to wait before it was on the scoreboard before I could believe I'd won,' he said, 'It was amazing to see my name come up first.' Pistorius was quick to offer his congratulations to his successor as champion. 'We just witnessed one of the great performances from Jonnie,' he said. 'He stepped up to the plate. We witnessed one of the great Paralympic performances.'

It had been an amazing night, exciting enough to rival anything seen at the Olympic Games. David Weir went on to win a magnificent fourth gold medal in the Marathon – T54, and yet Peacock's single victory in the only event he contested made him equally synonymous with those fabulous Paralympic Games. The performance of the teenager from Doddington, a village in Cambridgeshire, provided a wonderful example of what Lord Coe referred to in his Closing Ceremony speech as 'Paralympians lifting the cloud of limitation.'

Pistorius, meanwhile, who did win an individual gold medal in the 400m – T44, another gripping contest, recognised what he had been a part of on that 'Thrilling Thursday'. He called the 100m 'one of the best races I have ever been in', adding, 'there is something definitely happening in the Paralympic Movement that is making me emotional. I don't mind if I don't finish on the podium if the sport is getting better and better.' It is.

If there was a fitting finale to an amazing 11 days of Paralympic sport it came at the Closing Ceremony, when Peacock and the double gold medal-winning swimmer Ellie Simmonds were chosen to extinguish the Cauldron. The aim for the BPA between now and the next Paralympic Games at Rio de Janeiro in four years time will be to find more athletes like them to continue Great Britain's success after the team's 120 medals at London 2012. There will, however, only ever be one Jonnie Peacock.

About the Editor

Brendan Gallagher is the chief sports feature writer at the *Daily Telegraph*, specialising in basketball, rugby, cycling, athletics and cricket. He has co-authored the auto-biography of Ireland and Lions captain Brian O'Driscoll and, most recently, that of four times Olympic gold medal winner Bradley Wiggins, *In Pursuit of Glory*. A former director of Hayters Sports Agency, he has a particular interest in historical sporting events and the Olympic and Paralympic Games heritage.

Contributors

Kate Battersby began her working life with a secretarial stint at ITV's flagship sports programme World Of Sport where – in answer to the common question – she was not, alas, one of the girls typing on-screen behind Dickie Davies. As a journalist she joined the sportswriting staff of the *Daily* and *Sunday Telegraphs*. In 1996 she switched to the *Evening Standard* to become the first female chief sportswriter in Fleet Street. Now freelance, she has written on many sports for newspapers including the *Daily Mail*, the *Daily Express* and *The Sunday Times*. She was a contributor to this book's sister publication *Heat of the Moment*.

Pippa Cuckson is a former deputy editor of *Horse & Hound*. After a spell in the racing industry, she became a freelance writer. She became the *Daily Telegraph's* equestrian correspondent in 2009, also contributing to leading overseas titles *Chronicle of the Horse* and *Horse Sport International*. She writes on her other main interest, classical music, for *Country Life* and recently won *The Spectator's* inaugural prize for environmental journalism.

Gareth A Davies is an award-winning sports writer who has been Paralympics Correspondent for the *Telegraph Media Group* at the last four Paralympic Games. He is also Correspondent for Boxing and Mixed Martial Arts, and believes the spirit of the competitors is similar in all three sporting areas. The International Paralympic Committee bestowed the prestigious 'World Print Media Coverage Award' to the *Daily Telegraph* after its coverage of the Athens 2004 Games, and to the *Sunday Telegraph* after the Beijing 2008 Games. Davies was at the heart of the *Telegraph's* coverage.

Sarah Edworthy has over 20 years' varied experience in journalism, ranging from reviews of fiction at *The Times* to *Harpers & Queen* and the sports pages of the *Daily Telegraph*, including coverage of less familiar Olympic sports. A keen traveller with an eye for engaging stories, she is also the co-author of *El Macca: Four Years at Real Madrid* with Steve McManaman and *My Championship Year* with Jenson Button (2009).

Shelagh Fogarty presents the Lunchtime Show for BBC Five Live including a weekly live broadcast from Westminster for Prime Minister's Questions. Previously she co-presented Five Live's Breakfast show with Nicky Campbell, during which time they were multiple Sony Radio Award winners. She has anchored programmes from around the world covering some of the biggest stories of the past decade – most recently the Euro Crisis from Ireland, the Japanese earthquake and tsunami from Tokyo, and the Breivik massacre from Norway. She was live from Wimbledon for the whole of the famous tournament in 2012 and presented from various venues for the London 2012 Paralympic Games.

Tom Knight has been a journalist for more than 30 years and has covered nine Olympic Games. He has travelled extensively, writing about sport for a variety of newspapers and magazines and, for 10 years, was the *Daily Telegraph*'s athletics correspondent, with a portfolio that included sports politics and doping as well as a number of other Olympic events. Tom has contributed to *The Times*, *Guardian*, *Independent*, *Mail on Sunday*, *Daily Express* and the Press Association, and has appeared as an Olympic Games observer and athletics expert on Radio 2, Radio 5 Live, Talksport, Channel 4 and CNN.

Andrew Longmore is an award-winning writer on *The Sunday Times*, where he covers all the Olympic sports as well as football, cricket and racing. He has been Chief Sports Feature Writer at *The Times* and Chief Sports Writer at the *Independent on Sunday*. London 2012 was his fifth Summer Games, along with two

Winter Games, as well as football, rugby and cricket World Cups. Andrew's awards include Olympic Sports Reporter of the Year in 2000 and Sports Feature Writer of the Year in 2003. He has also writen several books, including a biography of jockey Kieren Fallon.

Craig Lord is a sports writer for *The Times* and *Sunday Times* and the senior correspondent for the specialist publication *SwimNews*. A former Deputy Editor of Times Online, he masterminded the Sydney 2000 Olympic Games online microsite for *The Times*. He has reported on the past six Olympic Games for the London-based news organisation. In 2007, Lord received the Al Schoenfield Media Award from the International Swimming Hall of Fame and in 2009 he was presented with the American Swimming Coaches Association Media Award.

Vikki Orvice has been a staff sports writer for the *Sun* for 17 years, specialising in football, athletics and the Olympic Games. She was the first woman to be appointed as a staff football writer on a British tabloid and has regularly appeared on radio and TV. She has covered European Championships and a World Cup as well as Wimbledon, the French Open, the Commonwealth Games, World Athletics Championships and London 2012, the fourth Olympic Games she has worked at. She was also in Singapore when London won the bid to host the 2012 Games and was the first woman to be elected chairman of the British Athletics Writer's Association.

Kevin Owens trained and practised in architecture prior to his role as Design Principal with the London Organising Committee of the Olympic Games and Paralympic Games. He studied architecture at Yale University as a Fulbright Scholar and has worked on a wide range of design projects, including The Hollywood Bowl redevelopment for the Los Angeles Philharmonic, Kensington Oval Cricket Ground Barbados, and Cambridge University Sports Centre, West Campus. At LOCOG Kevin led on the design of the built environment and provided the strategic direction on the design and overlay for all venues, in the Olympic

Park and elsewhere. He facilitated a single shared design ethos and strategy for London 2012, ensuring a holistic approach to all aspects of the built environment, from architecture and engineering to graphics and artwork.

Pat Rowley is a prolific writer on international hockey. A former author, journalist, radio and TV commentator, he has spent his later years concentrating on that sport. Former Assistant Sports Editor of the *Observer*, he also worked on numerous sports for the *Guardian* for over 50 years and *The Sunday Times* for a quarter of a century. He also edited *World Hockey*, the magazine of the International Hockey Federation, for 25 years and was a member of that body's committees.

Simon Turnbull has been athletics correspondent of the *Independent on Sunday* since 1996. He has also been athletics correspondent of the *Independent* since 2008. A former provincial sports writer of the year, he has been writing about athletics for national and international publications since 1980 and is vice-chairman of the British Athletics Writers' Association. A member of Blaydon Harriers on Tyneside, he is a former Durham County schools' sprint champion and has run a 2hr 50min marathon. He won awards for his coverage of the Seoul 1988 Olympic Games for the Thomson Regional Newspaper Group. London 2012 was his sixth summer Olympic Games.

Picture Credits

The publishers would like to thank the following for permission to reproduce the images in this book:

Plate section 1: 1 © ODA; 2 © Getty Images; 3 © Getty Images; 4 © Getty Images; 5 © Press Association for LOCOG; 6 © Press Association for LOCOG; 7 © Getty Images; 8 © Getty Images; 9 © Getty Images; 10 © Getty Images; 11 © Getty Images; 12 © Getty Images; 13 © Getty Images.

Plate section 2: 14 © Getty Images; 15 © Getty Images; 16 © Getty Images; 17 © Mike King; 18 © Getty Images; 19 © Getty Images; 20 © Getty Images; 21 © Getty Images; 22 © Getty Images; 23 © Mike King; 24 © Getty Images; 25 © Getty Images; 26 © Mike King.